Scholastic Writer's Desk Reference

Table of Contents

Part 1
Grammar

Parts of Speech

The eight parts of speech are the building blocks of sentences. When you learn to use the parts of speech correctly, your sentences will mean just what you want them to mean.

Nouns

What Is a Noun?

A **noun** is a word that names a person, animal, place, thing, or idea. There are more nouns in the English language than any other kind of word.

Persons	Animals	Places	Things	Ideas
teacher	shark	school	pen	concentration
student	hamster	gym	computer	wisdom
girl	fish	Lake Erie	mailbox	kindness
boy	aardvark	Chicago	skateboard	freedom
Mrs. Li	bear	village	tree	fear
Tanya	flea	Africa	cereal	love

A, an, and **the** are special words called **articles.** They are noun signals. They can often tip you off that there's a **noun** coming up in the sentence.

The noun could be the very next word after the article.

> *A clown ate the apple.*

Or it could be one or more words later.

> *A roly-poly, floppy-eared, hilariously funny clown ate the big, red, delicious apple.*

Kinds of Nouns

Singular and Plural Nouns

Singular means one of something. Plural means more than one.

Five Ways to Make Nouns Plural

1. **You can make most nouns plural by just adding s.**

one pencil	*four pencils*
one car	*a garage full of cars*

2. **If the noun ends with s, ch, sh, x, or z, add es to make it plural.**

one dress	*a rack of dresses*
one church	*three churches*
one brush	*a box of brushes*
one fox	*a den of foxes*
one buzz	*many buzzes of many bees*

3. **To make some nouns that end with f or fe plural, change the f to v and add es.**

knife	*knives*
half	*halves*
leaf	*leaves*

> *Not all nouns that end with f or fe follow this rule. For example, safe, waif, and bluff don't. But most do.*

4. **Add s if the letter in front of the y is a vowel, to make plural a noun that ends in y.**

toy	*toys*
key	*keys*

5. **Drop the y and add ies if the letter in front of the y is a consonant.**

dictionary	*dictionaries*
penny	*pennies*

Some nouns have tricky plurals.

one man	*a group of men*

Forty-one Irregular Plurals

Some nouns are not regular. When irregular nouns become plural, they change their spellings, or they stay the same, and a few even have more than one plural form. Here are forty-one of the trickiest irregular nouns with their plural forms.

Singular	Plural
alga	algae
alumna	alumnae
alumnus	alumni
antenna (on a television)	antennas
antenna (on a bug's head)	antennae
appendix	appendixes, appendices
bacterium	bacteria
bison	bison
buffalo	buffalos, buffaloes, buffalo
bus	buses, busses
cactus	cacti, cactuses
child	children
corps	corps
crisis	crises
datum	data
deer	deer
die	dice
dwarf	dwarfs, dwarves
foot	feet
fish	fish, fishes

goose	geese
half	halves
hippopotamus	hippopotami, hippopotamuses
hoof	hoofs, hooves
louse	lice
man	men
moose	moose
mouse	mice
octopus	octopi, octopuses, octopodes
ox	oxen
scarf	scarves, scarfs
series	series
sheep	sheep
staff (stick or line for charting music)	staves
staff (group of workers)	staffs
stegosaurus	stegosauri
swine	swine
talisman	talismans
tooth	teeth
wharf	wharfs, wharves
woman	women

Common and Proper Nouns

■ A common noun names any old, regular, ordinary person, animal, place, thing, or idea. Nothing specific.

■ A proper noun names a very specific, very particular person, animal, place, thing, or idea.

■ A proper noun always begins with a capital letter.

Common Nouns	Proper Nouns
woman	Harriet Tubman
boy	Aaron Leong
superhero	Batman
dog	Lassie
horse	Black Beauty
cat	Cheshire Cat
mountain	Mount Everest
river	Mississippi River
city	Boston
building	Astrodome
school	Columbia Middle School
house	Monticello
holiday	Fourth of July

Concrete and Abstract Nouns

■ A **concrete noun** names a person, animal, place, or thing that you can actually see, touch, taste, hear, or smell.

radio *spaghetti* *tuba* *onions* *fire*

muffins *perfume* *cloud*

■ An **abstract noun** names an idea, feeling, emotion, or quality.

beauty *happiness* *ability* *anger* *nature*

love *speed*

These things exist, but you cannot actually pick them up, hear them, taste them, smell them, or even see them in the real world. (You can see that someone is angry. You might be able to see what makes her angry. But you can't really see anger.)

Collective Nouns

A **collective noun** names a group of people, animals, or things. Here are some examples:

People		
audience	crew	cast
crowd	family	band
gang	group	choir
jury	chorus	nation
class	orchestra	quartet
club	quintet	committee
trio	duo	staff

Animals		
flock	herd	swarm
pack	brood	team
gaggle	colony	warren
school	pride	litter

Things		
bunch	set	cache
bundle	stack	batch
fleet	cluster	bouquet
pod	clump	clutch

Compound Nouns

A **compound noun** is made up of two or more words used together.

Compound nouns can be:

One Word	Two Words	Hyphenated
shoelace	seat belt	baby-sitter
flashlight	high school	self-awareness
applesauce	word processor	great-grandchild

If you can't remember if a compound noun is one word, two words, or hyphenated, check your dictionary.

Eight Uses of Nouns

1. *Subject of the Sentence*

The subject is the person, animal, place, thing, or idea that the sentence is about.

One way to find the subject is to ask yourself who or what is performing the action of the verb.

> The *teacher* laughed hysterically.

Which person is that sentence about? The teacher. Who laughed? The teacher. **Teacher** is the subject of the sentence.

> *Pencils* always break just before a big test.

What things is that sentence about? Pencils. What things always break? Pencils. **Pencils** is the subject of the sentence.

> *Enthusiasm* can be the difference between winning and losing.

What idea is that sentence about? Enthusiasm. What idea can be the difference? Enthusiasm. **Enthusiasm** is the subject of the sentence.

2. *Predicate Noun (or Predicate Nominative)*

A predicate noun comes after the verb **to be** and means the same thing as the subject of the sentence. (A predicate noun can also come after a linking verb: **to become, to remain**, etc.)

> My brother is the funniest *kid* in the world.

> Lorraine will become *chairperson* of the committee.

> I am the *boss,* and don't you forget it!

How to Identify a Predicate Noun

You can check to see if a word is a predicate noun by switching it with the subject. If the sentence still makes sense, that word is the predicate noun.

Ms. Youngman is the substitute math teacher today.

The substitute math teacher today is Ms. Youngman.

Ms. Youngman = teacher; teacher = Ms. Youngman. **Teacher** is the predicate noun in the first sentence above. **Ms. Youngman** is the predicate noun in the second sentence.

---

3. Appositive

An appositive is a word or phrase (group of words) that comes after another word and identifies, explains, or gives information about that word. The appositive word or phrase is set off from the rest of the sentence by one or two commas.

Tokyo, the capital of Japan, is a crowded city.

Give this robot dog to that tall woman, one of our secret agents.

The school janitor, Mr. Forest, turned on the radiators.

When one noun is the appositive for another noun, we sometimes say that they are "in apposition."

4. Direct Object of a Verb

The direct object is the person, animal, place, thing, or idea that receives the action of the verb.

Carlos locked the coach in the gym.

What's the action? Locking someone in. Which person got locked in? The coach. **Coach** is the direct object of the verb.

> *From the top of the skyscraper, Maria can hardly see the street.*

What's the action? Seeing something. What place can Maria hardly see? The street. **Street** is the direct object of the verb.

> *Superheroes fight injustice wherever they go.*

What's the action? Fighting an idea. What idea do superheroes fight? Injustice. **Injustice** is the direct object of the verb.

5. *Indirect Object of a Verb*

The **indirect object** receives the action of the verb—indirectly.

> *Should I send David some extra money?*

What am I sending? Some extra money. Who will receive the extra money (if I send it)? **David** is the indirect object.

Ways to Identify the Indirect Object

1. Imagine that **to** or **for** is in front of the indirect object.

   Should I send (to) David some extra money?

2. The indirect object always comes before the direct object. In the example above, **some extra money** is the direct object of the verb **should send**.

3. Some verbs are usually followed by indirect objects: **give, buy, throw, show, award, lend, save, bake, send,** and **knit**.

   Paloma tried to give (to) her teacher the message.

   Karen baked (for) Mrs. Freedman a carrot-raisin cake.

   Save (for) me a seat at the Killer Kanary concert.

6. Object of the Preposition

A **preposition** is a word that shows location, movement, or direction. Some common prepositions are **in, on, with, by, for,** and **under**.

A preposition is always followed by a noun (or pronoun) called the **object of the preposition**. Together, with the preposition, they form a **prepositional phrase**.

against the stormy sea

beneath a pile of dinosaur bones

during the Revolutionary War

into the raging volcano

under the table

7. Object Complement

An **object complement** is a word that completes the meaning of the direct object. **Complement** comes from the verb **to complete.** You use an object complement when the direct object wouldn't make complete sense by itself.

> *My grandfather named his cat Peaches.*

> *The country elected Lincoln president.*

Peaches and **president** are object complements. Without those words, you wouldn't know what name my grandfather gave to his cat or to what office Lincoln was elected.

8. To Show Possession

A **possessive noun** tells who or what owns (possesses) something.

> *The boy's hat is on the floor.*

Who owns the hat? The boy does. **Boy's** is a possessive noun.

> *Alaska's weather is much milder in the summer.*

What place's weather is milder in the summer? Alaska's is. **Alaska's** is a possessive noun.

How to Make Nouns Possessive

To make a singular noun possessive, just add 's.

president	the president's plane
ox	the ox's tale
boss	my boss's car
Holmes	Sherlock Holmes's violin

To make a plural noun possessive, check the last letter of the plural noun. If it's an s, just add an apostrophe.

girls	those girls' science kits
students	the students' book bags
gerbils	my gerbils' food

If the last letter of the plural noun is not s, add 's.

men	the men's shoes
mice	her mice's cheese
teeth	your teeth's enamel

If you know the ways nouns are used, you are less likely to make a mistake using a pronoun.

Pronouns

What Is a Pronoun?

A pronoun is a word that takes the place of a noun. Almost anything a noun can do, a pronoun can do, too. Pronouns are handy little words because when you use them, you don't have to keep repeating nouns all the time.

Without pronouns:

> *Jennifer said that Jennifer was going to give Jennifer's cats Jennifer's cats' food.*

With pronouns:

> *Jennifer said that she was going to give her cats their food.*

There are six kinds of pronouns: personal, demonstrative, indefinite, intensive, reflexive, and interrogative, but personal pronouns are the ones we use most.

Personal Pronouns

Personal pronouns refer to specific people and things. In order to use personal pronouns, it is important to know about case (subject, object, and possessive), number (singular or plural), and person (first, second, or third).

Subject, Object, and Possessive Cases

■ Subject Pronouns

> *I, you, he, she, it, we, they*

A subject pronoun is used as a subject or a predicate noun.

I am the lion tamer, and you are just the lion.

It was she who did that.

■ Object Pronouns

me, you, him, her, it, us, them

An **object pronoun** is used as an indirect object, direct object, or object of a preposition.

Dad told me to give him the cake.

The teacher saw you do it.

The boys are going with us and them.

Pronouns come in subject/object pairs:

Subject	Object
I	me
you	you
he	him
she	her
it	it
we	us
they	them

■ Possessive Pronouns

Possessive pronouns take the place of possessive nouns (nouns that show ownership).

Her sandwich is much thicker than his.

Lola's sandwich is much thicker than Larry's.

Possessive Pronouns	
my	mine
your	yours
his	
her	hers
its	
our	ours
their	theirs

Never put a noun right after **mine**, **yours**, **hers**, **ours**, and **theirs** because, by themselves, they take the place of possessive nouns.

*If this thing isn't **hers**, it must be **theirs**.*

***Yours** is much funnier-looking than **mine**.*

Seven Uses of Personal Pronouns

Pronouns are used to replace nouns in the following ways:

1. Subject of a sentence:

The boy ran for the school bus.

He ran for the school bus.

2. Predicate pronouns:

The leader of the troop is Dave.

The leader of the troop is he.

3. **Direct object of a verb:**

    I saw Karen at the mall.

    I saw her at the mall.

4. **Indirect object of a verb:**

    Try to sell Mr. and Mrs. Cejwin a glass of lemonade.

    Try to sell them a glass of lemonade.

5. **Object of a preposition:**

    The truckload of feathers fell on the two monkeys.

    The truckload of feathers fell on them.

> **1 and 2 use subject pronouns.**
> **3, 4, and 5 use object pronouns.**

6. **Appositive:**

    The new students, Tim and she, were asked to stand.

    Please take the advice of your friends, Jane and me.

7. **To show possession (ownership):**

    This is Mary, Paula, and Sybil's science project.

    This is their science project.

How to Choose the Correct Pronoun: Subject or Object?

Sometimes people don't know whether to use the subject or the object pronoun in sentences like these:

My brother and (I, me) went to the pet store.

Here the pronoun is a part of the subject, so use a subject pronoun.

My brother and I went to the pet store.

The principal saw Tamika and (I, me).

Here the pronoun is a direct object, so use an object pronoun.

The principal saw Tamika and me.

And remember, always put yourself last. Grammar is polite.

Quick Clue

Here's another way to pick the right pronoun. Take away the other words that go with **I** or **me**.

Me went to the pet store.

You can usually hear which pronoun is the right one. Now put the other words back.

My brother and I went to the pet store.

Try it with the other sample sentence below.

The principal saw Tamika and (I, me).

The principal saw I.

The principal saw me.

The principal saw Tamika and me.

This method works with all the other subject and object personal pronouns, too. Check it out.

How to Decide Between Who and Whom

Many people mix up **who** and **whom**. **Who** is a subject pronoun. When a sentence (or clause) needs a subject or a predicate nominative, use **who**.

Who will be watching?

The President of the United States is who?

I recognized the girl who was ice skating.

Whom is an object pronoun. When a sentence needs a direct object, indirect object, or object of a preposition, use **whom**.

Direct object: *Whom did you invite to the party?*

Indirect object: *You knitted whom a cashmere sweater?*

Object of the preposition: *To whom did you give the ring?*

If you really get confused about using **who** and **whom**, try this: In your mind, rewrite just the part of the sentence that contains **who** or **whom**. Instead of **who**, use **he**. Instead of whom, use him. See which one sounds better. If **him** sounds better, use **whom** in the original sentence. Otherwise, use **who**.

> *The boy (who, whom) we chose class president moved to Ohio.*
>
> **Try saying: We chose he. We chose him. Him sounds better, so it's:**
>
> *The boy whom we chose class president moved to Ohio.*
>
> *That is the boy (who, whom) is moving to Ohio.*
>
> **Try saying: He is moving. Him is moving. He sounds right, so it's:**
>
> *That is the boy who is moving to Ohio.*

Number

The "number" of a pronoun shows whether the pronoun refers to a single person or thing (singular) or to more than one person or thing (plural). Number is important because it tells you which verb to use—singular or plural.

Singular pronouns are **I, me, my, mine, he, she, him, her, his, hers, it,** and **its.**

Plural pronouns are **we, us, our, ours, they, them, their,** and **theirs.**

You and **yours** are both singular and plural.

First-Person, Second-Person, and Third-Person Pronouns

We also divide personal pronouns into three groups called persons.

1. First-person is the person speaking:

   I, we

   me, us

   my, mine, our, ours

2. Second-person is the person spoken to: *you, your, yours*

3. Third-person is the person or thing spoken about:

   he, she, it

   his, her, hers, its

   him, her, it

   they, them, their, theirs

Here is a chart that shows the personal pronouns by case, number, and person:

		Singular	Plural
1st-person	**subject**	*I*	*we*
	object	*me*	*us*
	possessive	*my, mine*	*our, ours*
2nd-person	**subject**	*you*	*you*
	object	*you*	*you*
	possessive	*your, yours*	*your, yours*
3rd-person	**subject**	*he, she, it*	*they*
	object	*him, her, it*	*them*
	possessive	*his, her, hers, its*	*their, theirs*

Five Other Kinds of Pronouns

1. Demonstrative Pronouns

Demonstrative pronouns point out (demonstrate) specific persons, animals, places, things, and ideas. There are only four of them.

this	*that*	*these*	*those*

Please exchange this for that and these for those.

This is the way to dress the baby for warm weather.

2. Indefinite Pronouns

Indefinite pronouns refer to nouns in a general, indefinite sort of way. Here's a list of words that can be used as indefinite pronouns.

all	another	any	anybody	anyone	anything
both	each	either	everybody	everyone	everything
few	many	neither	nobody	no one	nothing
one	others	several	some	somebody	someone
			something		

Everybody can do something, but nobody can do every-thing!

Many bought tickets to the show, but few actually came.

Some indefinite pronouns can also be used as **adjectives** (for example: **all, any, both, each, few, one, several,** and **some**). When these words are adjectives, they have nouns after them (**both** cats, **few** people, etc.). When they are indefinite pronouns, they have no nouns after them. (**Each** has his own book. **Both** knew the answer.)

3. Intensive Pronouns

Intensive pronouns emphasize (intensify) a noun or another pronoun. They really make you notice the nouns and pronouns they go with.

Singular	Plural
myself	ourselves
yourself	yourselves
himself	
herself	themselves
itself	

Kareem himself ordered the birthday cake.

Roxy went right up to the mayor herself and said, "Hi!"

4. Reflexive Pronouns

The very same pronouns that we call intensive pronouns can also be used as reflexive pronouns. They don't intensify; they refer back to (reflect) the subject of the sentence.

Fatima wanted to kick herself when she saw her mistake.

You'll have to ask yourself what you really want to do.

5. Interrogative Pronouns

Interrogative pronouns ask questions. There are only five of them.

what	*which*	*who*	*whom*	*whose*

I demand to know who did what to whom!

Which should I leave, and whose should I take?

Master List of All Pronouns

Here are all the pronouns—personal, demonstrative, indefinite, intensive, interrogative, and reflexive—in alphabetical order for easy reference:

all	*either*	*herself*
another	*everybody*	*him*
any	*everyone*	*himself*
anybody	*everything*	*his*
anyone	*few*	*I*
anything	*he*	*it*
both	*her*	*its*
each	*hers*	*itself*

Master List of All Pronouns (continued)

many	ourselves	this
me	several	those
mine	she	us
my	some	we
myself	somebody	what
neither	someone	which
nobody	something	who
none	that	whom
no one	their	whose
nothing	theirs	you
one	them	your
others	themselves	yours
our	these	yourself
ours	they	yourselves

Verbs

What Is a Verb?

A **verb** is a word that shows action or being. Whatever you're doing can be expressed by a verb.

> Without a verb, a group of words cannot be a sentence. A sentence can be as short as one word long, as long as that one word is a verb. **Go!,** **Stop!,** and **Eat!** are all perfectly good one-word sentences.

Verbs That Show Action

Action doesn't mean just physical action like to **jump, run, throw, scream, swim,** and **climb.** Action also means quiet, slow, peaceful actions, both physical and mental, like to **think, listen, sleep, read, look, breathe, hear, wonder,** and **dream.**

Main Verbs and Helping Verbs

What Is a Main Verb?

The **main verb** expresses the main action or state of being in the sentence.

*The principal **called** Julio into his office.*

*Julio **is** nervous.*

What Is a Helping Verb?

Helping verbs are nice and help the main verb express tenses. There are twenty-three of these verbs.

> *am, are, is, was, were, be, being, been*
>
>   *do, does, did*
>
>   *have, has, had*
>
>   *may, must, might*
>
>   *can, could, would, should*
>
>   *shall, will*

A main verb can have up to three helping verbs.

> *Rozzie was laughing so hard, she spilled her soda.*

> *Jose should have known the answer to the math question.*

> *Kim will have been waiting an hour by the time we get there.*

Notice that the verb to be can be a helping verb or a main verb, or even both in the same sentence. (What a verb!)

As the main verb: *We are so glad that you will be there.*
As a helping verb: *I am leaving this house this minute!*
As a helping verb and a main verb: *Miguel was being bad again.*

Verb Tenses

Tense means **time** in grammar. The tense of a verb tells you when the action of the verb takes place. There are six main tenses.

1. Present tense means now:

   I ride my bike this very minute.

2. Past tense means before now:

   I rode my horse the day before yesterday.

3. Future tense means not yet (but any time after now):

   I will ride my skateboard to school this morning.

4. Present perfect tense means started in the past and just recently finished or still going on:

   I have ridden my moped around the park three times (and I'm still riding it).

5. Past perfect tense means finished before some other past action:

   I had ridden my wagon for a mile before I fell off.

6. Future perfect tense means the action will be started and finished in the future:

   I will have ridden the camel for hours before I get there.

The Three Principal Parts of Verbs: Present, Past, and Past Participle

Every verb has three main parts called principal parts.

1. The present is used by itself for the present tense (I go) and with the helping verb **will** for the future tense (I will go).

2. The past is used for the past tense (I went).

3. The past participle is used with the helping verbs **have**, **has**, or **had** to form the three perfect tenses:

   present perfect (I have gone)

   past perfect (I had gone)

   future perfect (I will have gone)

Regular Verbs

Most verbs are regular. Regular verbs just add **d** or **ed** when they change principal parts from the present to the past to the past participle.

Present	Past	Past Participle (used with have, has, had)
Now I jump.	Yesterday I jumped.	I have jumped.
Now we skate.	Yesterday we skated.	We had skated.

Ninety Irregular Verbs

Irregular verbs form their past tenses and past participles in other unpredictable ways. Here are some of the most common of these tricky irregular verbs:

Present	Past	Past Participle
(Now I . . .)	*(Yesterday I . . .)*	*(I have or had . . .)*
arise	arose	arisen
awake	awoke or awaked	awaked or awoke
bear	bore	borne
beat	beat	beat
begin	began	begun
bind	bound	bound
bite	bit	bitten or bit
blow	blew	blown
break	broke	broken
bring	brought	brought
burst	burst	burst
buy	bought	bought
catch	caught	caught
choose	chose	chosen
cling	clung	clung
come	came	come
cut	cut	cut
deal	dealt	dealt
dive	dived or dove	dived
do	did	done
draw	drew	drawn
drink	drank	drunk
drive	drove	driven
eat	ate	eaten

Present	Past	Past Participle
fall	fell	fallen
fight	fought	fought
flee	fled	fled
fly	flew	flown
forbid	forbade or forbad	forbidden
forget	forgot	forgotten or forgot
freeze	froze	frozen
get	got	got, gotten
give	gave	given
go	went	gone
grow	grew	grown
hang (a picture)	hung	hung
hang (a person)	hanged	hanged
hide	hid	hidden or hid
hold	held	held
keep	kept	kept
know	knew	known
lay	laid	laid
leave	left	left
lend	lent	lent
lie	lay	lain
lose	lost	lost
meet	met	met
pay	paid	paid
read	read	read
rid	rid	rid

Present	Past	Past Participle
ride	rode	ridden
ring	rang	rung
rise	rose	risen
run	ran	run
say	said	said
see	saw	seen
set	set	set
shake	shook	shaken
shine (the sun)	shone	shone
show	showed	shown or showed
shrink	shrank or shrunk	shrunk
sing	sang	sung
sit	sat	sat
slay	slew	slain
slide	slid	slid
speak	spoke	spoken
spin	spun	spun
spring	sprang	sprung
stand	stood	stood
steal	stole	stolen
sting	stung	stung
stride	strode	stridden
strike	struck	struck
strive	strove	striven
swear	swore	sworn
swim	swam	swum

Present	Past	Past Participle
swing	swung	swung
take	took	taken
teach	taught	taught
tear	tore	torn
tell	told	told
think	thought	thought
throw	threw	thrown
wake	waked or woke	waked or woken
wear	wore	worn
wring	wrung	wrung
write	wrote	written

> **If a verb has more than one choice for a principal part (for example, waked or woken), you can use whichever one sounds better to you.**

The Verb "To Be" and Other Linking Verbs

A linking verb links the subject to other words in the sentence. Linking verbs do not show action. They just say that someone or something is, was, or will be.

To Be

The verb to be (sometimes called "the verb of being") is the most common, most popular, most used verb in the English language. You use this verb dozens of times every day without realizing it.

There are only eight forms of the verb **to be**:

am   are   is   was   were   be   being   been

The six tenses of the ever-popular verb **to be**:

Singular	*Plural*
Present Tense	
I am	*we are*
you are	*you are*
he, she, it is	*they are*
Past Tense	
I was	*we were*
you were	*you were*
he, she, it was	*they were*
Future Tense	
I will be	*you will be*
you will be	*you will be*
he, she, it will be	*they will be*
Present Perfect Tense	
I have been	*we have been*
you have been	*you have been*
he, she, it has been	*they have been*
Past Perfect Tense	
I had been	*we had been*

you had been	*you had been*
he, she, it had been	*they had been*

Future Perfect Tense

I will have been	*we will have been*
you will have been	*you will have been*
he, she, it will have been	*they will have been*

Linking Verbs

Here is a list of the most common linking verbs except for **to be:**

to seem	*to appear*	*to look*	*to sound*	*to feel*
to taste	*to grow*	*to remain*	*to smell*	*to become*

Linking verbs are never followed by direct objects. They are followed by nouns (called **predicate nouns**) or adjectives (called **predicate adjectives**).

■ Linking verbs followed by predicate nouns:

> *With that one act, he became a **hero.***

> *She remained Ping-Pong **champ** for four years.*

■ Linking verbs followed by predicate adjectives:

> *Grandma grows more **beautiful** each day.*

> *You seem awfully **quiet.** Do you feel **sick?***

■ Sometimes a verb that is a linking verb in one sentence can be an action verb in another. When it is an action verb, it will be followed by a direct object, not a predicate adjective or predicate noun.

Linking verb: *That doesn't **sound** right to me.*

Action verb: *Sound **the fire alarm!***

Linking verb: *The stew smells **delicious.***

Action verb: *Can you smell **the garlic in this stew?***

Linking verb: *I think my soup tastes **too salty.***

Action verb: *May I taste **some Bubblegum Delight yogurt?***

Linking verb: *The teacher looks **funny today, doesn't she?***

Action verb: *Come look **at my hairdo!***

Adjectives

What Is an Adjective?

An adjective is a word that tells us more about a noun or a pronoun. An adjective describes or modifies (limits the use of) a noun.

Adjectives Answer Three Questions

Adjectives usually answer three questions about the nouns they describe: 1) **what kind of?** 2) **how many?** 3) **which one?**

1. What kind of?

   Roslyn spotted a huge monster in the cave!

   What kind of monster? **Huge.**

2. How many?

   Six ice cream cones, please.

   How many cones? **Six.**

3. Which one (or which ones)?

   I'll take that dress.

   Which dress? **That** one.

Three Kinds of Adjectives

1. Demonstrative Adjectives

This, that, these, and **those** are called demonstrative adjectives. They point out (demonstrate) nouns. They always answer the question **which one(s)?**

These cookies taste great, but I wouldn't eat those muffins.

Which cookies taste great? Which muffins should I not eat?

This, that, these, and **those** can also act as pronouns. Demonstrative pronouns are not followed by nouns, as demonstrative adjectives are. They take the place of nouns.

Demonstrative adjectives:

Give me that comic book, and I'll give you this baseball card.

Demonstrative pronouns:

*Give me **that,** and I'll give you **this.***

2. Common Adjectives

A **common adjective,** like a common noun, is just a plain, ordinary, everyday adjective. It describes a noun in a general way. It is not capitalized (unless it's the first word in a sentence).

Here are some common examples of common adjectives:
busy   bitter   soft   colorful
cooperative   warm   blue   sunny
red   juicy   grumpy
invisible   wet   gross

3. Proper Adjectives

A proper adjective is made from a proper noun. It is always capitalized.

Proper Noun	Proper Adjective
China	Chinese
Ireland	Irish
Switzerland	Swiss
Mars	Martian
Queen Elizabeth I	Elizabethan
U.S. Constitution	Constitutional

Sometimes a proper noun doesn't change at all to become a proper adjective. (Remember, a word is an adjective when it describes a noun.)

She's a Hollywood actress with a Texas accent who loves Idaho potatoes, New England clam chowder, and Maine lobsters.

All proper nouns can be made into or used as proper adjectives.

Comparison of Adjectives: Positive, Comparative, and Superlative

Sometimes one person or thing is taller or bigger or faster than someone or something else. Sometimes one person or thing is the tallest or biggest or fastest of all. To show these comparisons, an adjective can be expressed three ways (called degrees).

Positive Degree (describing one)	Comparative Degree (comparing two)	Superlative Degree (comparing more than two)
great	greater	greatest
disgusting	more disgusting	most disgusting

How to Compare Adjectives

■ Add **er** and **est** to short adjectives of one syllable (and sometimes two syllables).

short	shorter	shortest

■ If a one- or two-syllable adjective ends with a consonant and **y,** change the **y** to **i,** then add **er** and **est.**

happy	happier	happiest
ugly	uglier	ugliest

■ If a short adjective ends with **e,** just add **r** and **st.**

little	littler	littlest

■ Put **more** and **most** in front of longer adjectives (two, three, or more syllables).

alert	more alert	most alert
beautiful	more beautiful	most beautiful
interesting	more interesting	most interesting

Whether to add **er** and **est** or to use **more** and **most** can be tricky. In most cases, you can trust your ears. When in doubt, check your dictionary.

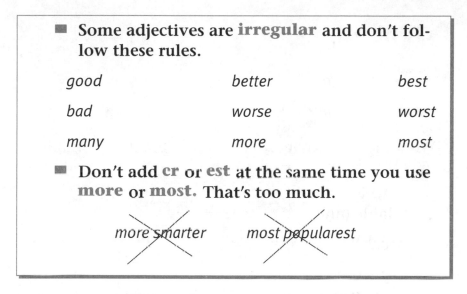

- Some adjectives are **irregular** and don't follow these rules.

good	*better*	*best*
bad	*worse*	*worst*
many	*more*	*most*

- Don't add **er** or **est** at the same time you use **more** or **most**. That's too much.

more smarter   *most popularest*

Where an Adjective Goes in a Sentence

Usually an adjective comes in front of the noun it is describing.

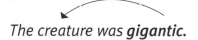

*The **gigantic** creature was hiding in the **scary** cave.*

But an adjective can also come after a linking verb, like **to be**, and describe the subject of the sentence. Then it's called a **predicate** adjective.

*The creature was **gigantic.***

Adverbs

What Is an Adverb?

An adverb is a word that tells us more about 1) a verb, 2) an adjective, or 3) another adverb.

We sometimes say that an adverb describes or modifies (limits the meaning of) these words.

When Adverbs Describe Verbs

Adverbs answer three questions about the verbs they describe: 1) how? 2) when? 3) where?

1. How?

> *The pig danced terribly.*

How did the pig dance? **Terribly.**

There are hundreds of adverbs that tell **how.** Here are some examples:

Adverbs that tell how:			
badly	fast	stupidly	brilliantly
loudly	gracefully	cleverly	quietly
vigorously	eagerly	skillfully	well
easily	slowly	wildly	too

2. Where?

> *The pig danced here.*

Where did she dance? **Here.**

Some other adverbs that tell where:					
above	down	inside	anywhere	everywhere	outside
away	here	there	backward	near	up

Some of these adverbs that tell where can also be used as prepositions:

> ***near** the boat*
>
> ***up** the stairs*

3. When?

> *The pig danced yesterday.*

When did she dance? **Yesterday.**

Some other adverbs that tell when:				
before	immediately	sometimes	daily	late
soon	periodically	lately	suddenly	eventually
never	then	finally	now	today
first	often	tomorrow	forever	seldom
tonight	frequently	yesterday	never	early

You can even put adverbs that answer different questions about the same verb together in one sentence.

> *The pig danced **terribly here yesterday.***

When Adverbs Describe Adjectives

Adverbs usually answer the question "how?" when they describe adjectives.

There are two adjectives in the sentences below, **ugly** and **old.**

Without adverbs: *My ugly dog likes old bones.*

With adverbs: *My extremely ugly dog likes very old bones.*

How ugly is my dog? **Extremely.** How old are the bones? **Very.**

Here are more examples of adverbs describing adjectives:			
really funny	*quite lovely*	*historically important*	*fully aware*
terribly bad	*fairly heavy*	*somewhat depressed*	*too tall*
rather sticky	*amazingly good*	*annoyingly loud*	*not fair*

When Adverbs Describe Other Adverbs

In the sentences below, **quickly** is an adverb. The words in italics (the slanted words) are also adverbs. They are modifying **quickly** and are answering the questions "how?" or, more exactly, "by how much?"

He eats quickly.

He eats *so* quickly.

He eats *too* quickly.

He eats *very* quickly.

He eats *quite* quickly.

He eats *rather* quickly.

He eats *really* quickly.

He eats *awfully* quickly.

He eats *somewhat* quickly.

He eats *extremely* quickly.

He eats *amazingly* quickly.

He eats *exceedingly* quickly.

He eats *extraordinarily* quickly.

(He's going to get sick *unbelievably* quickly!)

How to Change an Adjective into an Adverb

Many (but not all) adverbs end with the letters ly. You can often change an adjective into an adverb by adding ly.

soft + ly = softly   awful + ly = awfully

The three most common adverbs used in English are **not, very,** and **too.**

Comparison of Adverbs: Positive, Comparative, and Superlative

Adverbs can be compared just like adjectives.

Positive Degree (to modify one word)	Comparative Degree (to compare two words)	Superlative Degree (to compare more than two)
soon	sooner	soonest
rapidly	more rapidly	most rapidly

Glenn walks rapidly. His father walks more rapidly (than Glenn does). His grandfather walks most rapidly of the three.

Prepositions

What Is a Preposition?

A preposition is a word that shows the relationship of one word in a sentence to another word. The four things that prepositions tell are 1) **where something is** (location); 2) **where something is going** (direction); 3) **when something happens** (time); and 4) the **relationship** between a noun or a pronoun and another word in a sentence.

Four Things Prepositions Tell

1. Location

Many prepositions tell where something is in relation to something else.

> Amanda's guinea pig is *outside* its cage.

Other prepositions that show location are: **in, on, near, under,** and **inside.**

2. Direction

Other prepositions tell where something is going.

> Amanda's guinea pig ran *to* her cage.

Other prepositions that tell direction are: **around, toward, through, past,** and **beside.**

3. Time

A few prepositions help to tell time in a sentence.

> I'll wait *until* noon, and then I'm leaving.

> *During* the carnival, Simon lost his shoe.

4. Relationship

Other prepositions show the relationship between a noun (or pronoun) and another word.

Sasha went to the Halloween party **with** *Shana.*

This exciting book was written **by** *Mark Twain.*

Master List of One-Word Prepositions

aboard	below	in	since
about	beneath	inside	through
above	beside	into	throughout
across	besides	like	till
after	between	near	to
against	beyond	of	toward
along	but	off	under
alongside	by	on	underneath
among	despite	onto	until
around	down	out	up
as	during	outside	upon
at	except	over	with
before	for	past	within
behind	from	round	without

Some of the words on this list are not always prepositions. For example, **about, since,** and **until** can also be conjunctions. It depends on how the word is used in a particular sentence.

Compound Prepositions

Compound prepositions are two or more words working together like a one-word preposition. Here are some examples:

according to	in back of
ahead of	in case of
along with	in front of
as for	in regard to
away from	in spite of
because of	instead of
by way of	out of
due to	up to
except for	with the exception of
in addition to	

Every teacher with the exception of Ms. Blumenthal is out sick.

Every teacher **except** Ms. Blumenthal is out sick.

Prepositional Phrases

A prepositional phrase is a group of two or more words that begins with a preposition and ends with a noun or pronoun called the object of the preposition. Every preposition has an object.

Sometimes the object of the preposition is the very next word after the preposition:

Preposition	Object of the Preposition
near	*me*
at	*school*
with	*Eddie*

Or, it can come a few words later.

Preposition		Object of the Preposition
in spite of	*the terrible*	*weather*
inside	*the man's jacket*	*pocket*
throughout	*his long and illustrious*	*career*

A prepositional phrase includes the preposition, the object of the preposition, and all words in between.

You can have as many prepositional phrases in a sentence as you need. For example, here's the first line of a well-known song.

> *Over the river and through the woods to Grandmother's house we go.*

Conjunctions

What Is a Conjunction?

A conjunction is a word that joins other words or parts of sentences together. Conjunctions are like glue.

- Here are examples of conjunctions joining words together:

   David and Jennifer are brother and sister.

   The weather forecaster predicted snow or sleet today.

- Here are examples of conjunctions joining parts of a sentence together:

   I ran as fast as I could; however, I still missed the pie-throwing contest.

   I'll call the Department of Sanitation if you don't get that filthy animal out of here.

Kinds of Conjunctions

■ Coordinating Conjunctions

Coordinating conjunctions join words, phrases, and sentences (independent clauses) together.

and	nor	but	for	yet	so	or

■ Subordinating Conjunctions

A subordinating conjunction joins a dependent clause to an independent clause.

after	before	so	till	where
although	for	so that	unless	whereas
as	if	than	until	wherever
as if	once	that	when	whether
because	since	though	whenever	while

While you mind the baby, I'm going shopping.

I'm never talking to him again *unless* he tells me the secret.

A few of these same words can be used as prepositions in other sentences.

since yesterday   **after** the swim meet   **until** graduation

for her sake   **before** the judge   **till** tomorrow

■ *Correlative Conjunctions*

Correlative conjunctions are used in pairs, but the pair is split up by other words.

both/and	either/or	neither/nor
whether/or	just as/so	not only/but also

Both the giraffe *and* the chimpanzee have the hiccups.

Either you give me that letter *or* I'll tell the mailman.

Neither the mother *nor* the father knows about the cat.

Adverbial Conjunctions (Conjunctive Adverbs)

Adverbial conjunctions join clauses of equal value. They are like coordinating conjunctions because they join independent clauses together to make compound sentences.

accordingly	*consequently*	*moreover*
hence *however*	*nevertheless*	*therefore*

To learn how to punctuate sentences with adverbial conjunctions, see page 102.

Master List of Conjunctions

after	*but*	*not only/but also*	*unless*
although	*either/or*	*once*	*until*
and	*even though*	*or*	*when*
as	*for*	*since*	*whenever*
as if	*however*	*so*	*where*
as soon as	*if*	*so that*	*whereas*
as though	*in order that*	*than*	*wherever*
because	*just as/so*	*that*	*whether*
before	*neither/nor*	*though*	*while*
both/and	*nor*	*till*	*yet*

Interjections

What Is an Interjection?

Interjections are special words that show strong feelings or emotions like excitement, happiness, horror, shock, sadness, pain, anger, and disgust. Interjections usually come at the beginning of a sentence. You use them to add punch or energy to stories. Don't use them too much. When you overdo interjections, they lose their power.

Sometimes interjections are just sounds, shouts, gasps, or exclamations, more like noises than regular words.

Here are some common interjections:				
Aha	Gosh	Whoopee	Super	Yoo-hoo
Ahem	Hello	Oh	Ugh	Gee whiz
All right	Help	Oh, no	Well	Good grief
Dear me	Hey	Oops	Nuts	Right on
Gadzooks	Hooray	Ouch	Wow	Yippee
My goodness	Indeed	Phew	Yikes	Yuck

By the way, you can make up your own energetic interjections like:

Horsefeathers! She fell off the bronco.

Yazoo! The tornado is over.

Greasy grasshoppers! This street is slippery.

Sentences

There are four kinds of sentences. The chart below shows what they are called, what they do, and what punctuation mark to put at the end of each. Examples follow.

Kind of sentence	What it does	Final punctuation mark
Declarative	States a fact or makes a comment	Period
Interrogative	Asks a question	Question mark
Imperative	Gives a command or makes a request	Period (for a request or a mild order) or an exclamation mark (for a strong command)
Exclamatory	Expresses a strong emotion	Exclamation mark

Declarative:
He was born on Valentine's Day.

Interrogative:
Does his sister design unusual jewelry?

Imperative:
Pass the lizard sauce, please.
Put that tooth down this minute!

Exclamatory:
The jelly-making machine exploded!

Three Ways to Build a Sentence

In English there are three basic sentence structures: simple, compound, and complex.

1. Simple Sentences

A **simple sentence** is made up of one complete subject and one complete predicate. A simple sentence can be short or long.

> *She ate.*

> *My grandmother's neighbor from across the hallway ate a whole pot of spaghetti and meatballs by herself!*

The sentence is still simple even if the subject or the predicate is a compound.

> *Mom and Dad sang and danced.*

2. Compound Sentences

A **compound sentence** is made up of two or more independent clauses (simple sentences). These independent clauses are joined by a comma and a conjunction.

> *She asked me to the dance, and I said yes.*

> *You eat this banana and peanut butter sandwich, or I'll never make you lunch again.*

Conjunctions that join independent clauses are called **coordinating conjunctions.** The three that are used most often are **and, or,** and **but.**

Sometimes you can use a semicolon to join independent clauses instead of a comma and a conjunction.

The mechanical dinosaur in the museum had a short circuit; it started to dance!

3. Complex Sentences

A complex sentence contains an independent clause and a dependent clause. The two clauses are joined by a subordinating conjunction.

We'll just have to wait here until the spaceship comes.

Whenever I see that monkey, I think of my counselor at camp.

Notice that in the last sentence above, the dependent clause (the one that begins with the subordinating conjunction **whenever**) comes at the beginning of the sentence. In a complex sentence it doesn't matter which comes first, the independent or dependent clause. That sentence could have been written

I think of my counselor at camp whenever I see that monkey.

When a Group of Words Is Not a Sentence

Fragments

A fragment is not quite a whole sentence because it is missing either the subject or the main verb. Even if the group of words begins with a capital letter and has a punctuation mark at the end, it is still a fragment if either the subject or the main verb is missing.

Slipping down the muddy bank and plopping into the river.

Who is slipping and plopping? The subject is missing.

Belinda, who came all the way from South Africa by plane.

What about her? What did she do? The predicate is missing.

How to Fix Fragments

Put in the missing subject or predicate so that the sentence makes complete sense, or take out a word that is keeping it from being a complete sentence.

A hippo in a tutu was slipping on the muddy bank and plopping into the river.

Belinda came all the way from South Africa by plane.

Belinda, who came all the way from South Africa by plane, had never seen snow before.

Run-ons

A run-on sentence is really two or more sentences (or in-dependent clauses) that run together without the proper punctuation to join them.

It may rain today take your umbrella.

At first that may look like one sentence, but it's really two independent clauses with no punctuation to join them together.

How to Fix a Run-on Sentence

First, decide what the separate sentences are. Where does the first sentence end, and where does the second sentence begin?

It may rain today   take your umbrella

Then fix the run-on sentence in one of three ways:

1. Join the two sentences with a comma and a conjunction.

   It may rain today, so take your umbrella.

(A comma by itself is not strong enough to join the two parts together. You must use both a comma and a conjunction.)

2. Join the two sentences with a semicolon.

   It may rain today; take your umbrella.

3. Make two separate sentences.

   It may rain today. Take your umbrella.

Making Subjects and Verbs Work Together: Subject-Verb Agreement

The **subject** and **verb** in a sentence must be the same (agree) in person (1st, 2nd, or 3rd) and in number (singular or plural).

■ A **first-person** subject takes a first-person verb.

   I am the cheese.

- A second-person subject takes a second-person verb.

    You are going to get into trouble for this.

- A third-person subject takes a third-person verb.

    Marilyn is not allowed to stay up that late.

- A singular subject takes a singular verb.

    The porcupine sneezes.

- A plural subject takes a plural verb.

    The porcupines sneeze.

In most cases your ear can be the judge of whether or not the subject and verb match up.

Subject and verb do not agree:
We has never been here before.

Subject and verb agree:
We have never been here before.

Subject-Verb Agreement Example: To Run

Here is the verb **to run** matched up with all the personal pronoun subjects to show how a subject and a verb agree (are the same) in person and number.

Singular
1st person: I run, am running, was running, do run, did run, etc.
2nd person: you run, are running, were running, do run, did run, etc.
3rd person: he, she, it runs, is running, was running, does run, did run, etc.

Plural
1st person: we run, are running, were running, do run, did run, etc.
2nd person: you run, are running, were running, do run, did run, etc.
3rd person: they run, are running, were running, do run, did run, etc.

Verbs with Collective Nouns

A collective noun is usually followed by a **singular verb** because the group usually acts together as a single unit.

*My class **has seen** this movie.*

*The flock of geese **flies** south every winter.*

*This set of tapes **is** on sale this week.*

But sometimes a collective noun can be plural. That happens when members of the group are acting as separate individuals, not as a single unit.

Singular: *The team is coming onto the field now.*

Plural: *The team are unable to make up their minds.*

In the first sentence above, the people on the team are all doing the same thing together, so the collective noun (**team**) is singular and is followed by a singular verb (**is coming**).

In the second sentence above, the individual members of the team are not all acting together. **Team** here means separate people, not a single unit. That's why **team** takes a plural verb (**are**).

Verbs with Compound Subjects Joined by And

Compound subjects are plural when they are joined by **and.**

The duck and the goose were splashing in the pond.

Sometimes we use two food words together so often that we think of them as one dish.

peanut butter and jelly   *bacon and eggs*

When words like these are the subjects of a sentence, make the verb singular.

Macaroni and cheese is my favorite lunch.

Bread and water was all the prisoner got to eat.

Verbs with Compound Subjects Joined by Or

When compound subjects are joined by **or**, the verb matches the subject that follows **or**. That subject could be singular or plural.

> Here is an easy way for you to decide whether the verb should be singular or plural. Leave out all the rest of the words in the sentence except the subject after **or** and the verb. If they sound right together, put the rest of the words back.
>
> *Either my dog or I am responsible for this accident.*
> (**Check:** I am responsible . . .)
>
> *Either you or your dog is responsible for this accident.*
> (**Check:** Your dog is responsible . . .)
>
> *Either she or her dogs are responsible for this accident.*
> (**Check:** Her dogs are responsible . . .)

Indefinite Pronouns: Singular or Plural

Some indefinite pronouns are singular. Some are plural. A few are both!

Singular:

another	*everybody*	*no one*
anybody	*everyone*	*nothing*
anyone	*everything*	*one*
anything	*much*	*somebody*
each	*neither*	*someone*
either	*nobody*	*something*

Each (one) *of the animals makes a different sound.*

Neither (one) *of his parents is coming to the game.*

Plural:

both   few   many   others   several

Both are rock stars.

Many have known this weird story.

Either singular or plural:

all   any   most   none   some

These pronouns are plural when they refer to nouns (or pronouns) that can be counted one by one. They are singular when they refer to nouns (or pronouns) that cannot be counted.

Singular:

All of his allowance was spent on junk.

Plural:

All of his clothes were in the laundry.

Singular:

Some of this book is boring.

Plural:

Some of these books are from the library.

Singular:

Most of the video was out of focus.

Plural:

Most of the nuts were eaten by the monkey.

Preventing Double Negatives

Negative Words

Negative means **no**. A negative word expresses a meaning that is the opposite of positive. It says that something is not, rather than that something is.

Negative Word	Positive Opposite
no	yes, any
nobody	somebody, anybody
nothing	something, anything
nowhere	somewhere, anywhere
none	some, any
never	sometimes, often, ever
no one	someone, anyone
nor	or
neither	either
not	is

Although most negative words begin with an **n**, **hardly**, **scarcely**, and **barely** are also negative.

Negative Contractions

Not is one of the most frequently used negative words. The contraction for **not** is **n't**, so any contraction that ends in **n't** is a negative word.

aren't	can't	couldn't	didn't
doesn't	don't	hasn't	hadn't
haven't	isn't	mustn't	shouldn't
wasn't	weren't	wouldn't	won't (positive: will)

Ways to Prevent Double Negatives

Use only one negative word in a sentence to convey a negative meaning. If you say

> *Nobody wants none of your pie.*

you are really saying that everybody wants some of the pie. Two negatives make a positive.

Two Ways to Correct a Double Negative

1. Change a negative word into a positive word. If there is a negative contraction, you can either take it out of the sentence or drop the **n't** at the end.

Double negative:	*They don't have nothing to wear to the party.*
Correct sentences:	*They don't have anything to wear to the party.*
	They have nothing to wear to the party.
Double negative:	*She can't tell nobody about this.*
Correct sentences:	*She can't tell anybody about this.*
	She can tell nobody about this.

2. To correct double negatives that contain **hardly**, **barely**, or **scarcely**, change the other negative word into a positive word.

Double negative:	*She had hardly nothing left of her sandwich.*
Correct sentence:	*She had hardly anything left of her sandwich.*

Contractions: Shrinking Words

A contraction is one word that was once two. When you make a contraction, you squeeze together (or contract) two words into one.

Contractions help speed up your speaking and make it sound more natural. You can also use contractions in your writing, especially in a letter to a friend or when you write conversations, dialogue, or direct quotations. However, try not to use contractions too much in reports, research papers, and more formal writing.

How to Make a Contraction

To make a contraction, you leave out one or more letters from the original two words and replace them with an apostrophe ('). Put the apostrophe exactly in the place of the missing letter or letters.

Common Contractions

Contractions		Pronouns + Verbs
I'm	=	*I am*
I'd	=	*I would; I had*
I'll	=	*I will*
I've	=	*I have*
you'll	=	*you will*
you'd	=	*you would; you had*
you've	=	*you have*
you're	=	*you are*
he'll	=	*he will*
he'd	=	*he would; he had*
he's	=	*he is; he has*
she'll	=	*she will*
she'd	=	*she would; she had*
she's	=	*she is; she has*
it'll	=	*it will*
it'd	=	*it would; it had*
it's	=	*it is; it has*
we've	=	*we have*
we'd	=	*we would; we had*
we'll	=	*we will*
we're	=	*we are*
they'll	=	*they will*
they'd	=	*they would; they had*
they've	=	*they have*
they're	=	*they are*
who's	=	*who is; who has*
who'd	=	*who would; who had*

that'll	=	*that will*
that'd	=	*that would; that had*
that's	=	*that is; that has*
let's	=	*let us (verb + pronoun)*

Contractions   Verb + *not*

aren't	=	*are not*
can't	=	*cannot*
couldn't	=	*could not*
didn't	=	*did not*
doesn't	=	*does not*
don't	=	*do not*
hadn't	=	*had not*
hasn't	=	*has not*
haven't	=	*have not*
Isn't	=	*is not*
mustn't	=	*must not*
shouldn't	=	*should not*
wouldn't	=	*would not*
wasn't	=	*was not*
weren't	=	*were not*
won't	=	*will not*

Contractions   There + verb

there's	=	*there is; there has*
there'd	=	*there would; there had*
there'll	=	*there will*
there've	=	*there have*

Contractions   Words + *is* and *has*

what's	=	*what is; what has*
that's	=	*that is; that has*
who's	=	*who is; who has*
here's	=	*here is*

Building Compound Words

A compound word is made up of two or more words. Sometimes one word isn't enough to express an idea, name an object, or say what a speaker or writer is trying to express, so people make up compound nouns and adjectives. Compounds come three ways:

- **closed:** written as one word

- **open:** words written separately

- **hyphenated:** words joined by a hyphen (a short line)

Here are some common compound nouns and adjectives:

Closed Compounds	Open Compounds	Hyphenated Compounds
backyard	best seller	air-conditioned
barefoot	box office	all-purpose
blueberry	cough drop	best-selling
bookstore	day care	break-in
classmate	dining room	check-in
flashlight	hair coloring	drive-in
granddaughter	high school	entry-level
greenhouse	life preserver	follow-up
homework	milk shake	full-length
motorcycle	pencil sharpener	left-handed
paperback	post office	long-distance
textbook	seat belt	play-by-play
touchdown	study hall	tax-free

These words are usually written with hyphens:

- All fractions written out in words:

  one-half   *two-thirds*   *five-eighths*   *three-fourths*

- All two-word numbers from twenty-one to ninety-nine written out as words:

  thirty-three   *fifty-six*   *forty-nine*   *ninety-five*

- Most compounds that begin with **self:**

  self-employed   *self-esteem*   *self-taught*   *self-control*

- Some two- or three-word family members:

  great-aunt   *mother-in-law*   *great-grandfather*

How to Make Compound Nouns Plural

- **To make most one-word and two-word compound nouns plural, just add s to the end:**

  briefcases *boyfriends* *covered wagons* *launch pads*

- **With hyphenated compound nouns, make the most important word plural:**

  great-grandsons   *sisters-in-law*   *ladies-in-waiting*

Part 2
Punctuation

Punctuation Rules Everybody Needs

Apostrophes

Use apostrophes:

- in contractions.

    I'm sorry that she's coming after you've left.

- in possessive nouns.

    Sybil's cousin found Doug's umbrellas in the Goldins' car.

- when you refer to the plural of letters and words.

    *There are four **s**'s, four **i**'s, and two **p**'s in Mississippi.*

    *You have too many **very**'s in your essay.*

Capital Letters

To capitalize means to begin a word with a capital letter.

Capitalize the first word in a sentence.

The bunny ate too much, got dizzy, and fell off the sofa.

Capitalize the pronoun I.

*He had the nerve to say that **I** sang off key—**I**, who took singing lessons with Madame Margo for five years!*

Capitalize proper nouns (names of specific people, places, and things).

> *Roslyn Penn*
>
> *Columbia Prep School*
>
> *Brooklyn, New York*
>
> *Rocky Mountains*

Capitalize proper adjectives.

Proper adjectives come from proper nouns.

Proper Noun	Proper Adjective
America	American
Switzerland	Swiss
Japan	Japanese
Norway	Norwegian
Argentina	Argentine or Argentinean
Florida	Floridian
Boston	Bostonian

Capitalize ideas and abstract nouns when they are used as proper nouns for special effect (sometimes in poems, speeches, fables, myths, fairy tales, names of paintings, words of songs, or folktales).

O Freedom, how we do cherish thee!

What is life, without Liberty?

And then Mercy whispered tenderly, "I grant you pardon."

Capitalize official titles or positions when they come in front of a person's name.

Dr. Albert Schweitzer

Vice President Margaret Scotto

General Ulysses S. Grant

Chief Justice John Marshall

Ms. Lorrie Gerson

Prime Minister Margaret Thatcher

Captain Sue Kilmer

Professor Anthony Barnes

Capitalize important titles, even if the person's name is not mentioned.

The President of the United States went to the circus.

The Prime Minister forgot his hat at the conference.

We will have to consult the Secretary of Education on this.

Capitalize official titles when they are used without the person's name if you are speaking or writing directly to that person.

I must request, Judge, that you stop chewing on the gavel.

Yes, **G**overnor, I'll wipe the mustard off your tie immediately.

The war is that way, **G**eneral.

Look, **Y**our **M**ajesty, a hideous dragon is knocking at the gates of your castle. Shall I serve tea?

Capitalize abbreviations of titles after someone's name.

Martin Luther King, **Jr.**

Esther Brill, **Ph.D.**

Jason Brett, **M.D.**

Capitalize the titles of family members when they are used with their names.

Aunt Rozzie, **G**randpa Lester, **C**ousin Judi, **U**ncle Daisuke

Capitalize the titles of family members if you are speaking or writing directly to them, even if you don't use their names.

Thanks for the beautiful iguana, **G**randma.

Oh, **M**om and **D**ad, this is my new boyfriend, Rocko.

Capitalize the titles of specific family members if you are speaking about them without using their names. (It's as if their titles are their names.)

I heard **G**randma tell **D**ad that she had bought **M**om a new armadillo and that **G**randpa was jealous.

Capitalize the days of the week.

Monday, Tuesday, Wednesday, etc.

Capitalize the months of the year.

January, February, March, etc.

Do not capitalize the names of the seasons.

summer, fall, autumn, winter, spring

Capitalize the first word in the greeting (salutation) of a friendly letter.

My dear Angelo,   Hi, George,

Hello, Sayaka,   Dearest nephew Justin,

Dear Loraine,   Darling Amanda,

Capitalize the first word and all the main words in the greeting (salutation) of a business letter.

Dear Members of the Improvement Committee:

Dear Sir or Madam:

To Whom It May Concern:

Dear Customer Service Department:

Capitalize the first word in the closing of any letter, friendly or business.

Warmest wishes,   Your obedient servant,

Best regards,   Very truly yours,

Sincerely yours,   Fondly,

Love,   Respectfully,

Capitalize the first, last, and all the main words in titles.

book: *The Secret Garden*

movie: *Star Wars*

song: *"This Land Is My Land"*

play: *The Taming of the Shrew*

musical show: *The Lion King*

opera: *The Marriage of Figaro*

magazine: *Highlights for Children*

newspaper: *The New York Times*

television show: *I Love Lucy*

radio program: *World News Tonight*

Do not capitalize a short word (like the, a, an, of, in, by, or for) unless it is the first or last word in a title.

For Whom the Bell Tolls   *The Wizard of Oz*

Of Mice and Men   *Time Goes By*

A Tale of Two Cities   *Jumping In*

Capitalize the first word in most lines of poetry.

Birds, birds everywhere,

In the trees and in my hair;

Birds are fowl, but some are fair;

A bird is sitting in my chair!

Capitalize the names of languages.

French, Latin, Spanish

Capitalize the names of school subjects when they are specific courses listed in a school or college catalog. (Capitalize the first, last, and all important words.)

Environmental Issues	Greek and Roman Comedy
World History 101	Introduction to Advanced Math
Kitchen Chemistry	Painting and Drawing
Computer Repairs	Long-lost Literature

Do not capitalize school subjects that are not languages or specific courses in a school catalog or college listing.

math	geography
science	music
history	physical education
biology	art

Capitalize geographic locations when they refer to specific places on the map or sections of a country, not just directions.

Specific geographic locations (capitalize the first letter):

Henny went out **W**est to seek his fortune in oil wells.

Sun-Sook Kim and Alan moved from the **N**orth to the **S**outh.

Many great colleges are located in the **E**ast.

The Southwest can be very hot.

Directions (do not capitalize):

Drive south for two miles. Turn east at the traffic light and go one block. Drive north for two blocks. Turn west at the fountain, and you'll find the restaurant. But it's closed.

Capitalize holidays, festivals, and special events (national, regional, local, neighborhood, school, and religious).

All Saints' Day	*Labor Day*
Christmas	*Memorial Day*
Broadway Street Fair	*Monte Azul*
Columbus Day	*National Dog Week*
Easter	*Passover*
Eid el-Fitr	*Rosh Hashanah*
Flag Day	*Saint Patrick's Day*
Good Friday	*Shavuot*
Halloween	*Saint Andrew's Day*
Hanukkah	*Sukkot*
Homecoming Weekend	*Thanksgiving*
Id al-Adha	*Valentine's Day*
Id al-Fitr	*Veterans Day*
Kwanzaa	*Yom Kippur*

Capitalize religions, tribes, ethnic groups, and nationalities.

> African, Apache, Asian, Aztec, Buddhist, Caucasian, Cherokee, Christian, Hindu, Hispanic, Hopi, Irish-American, Islam, Israeli, Japanese, Jewish, Muslim, Pueblo, Romanian, Russian, Spanish, Swahili

Capitalize gods and goddesses and holy books and documents.

Allah	Brahma	Buddha	Vishnu
Bible	God	the Koran	New Testament
Old Testament	Shiva	Talmud	Torah

Capitalize the names of all the planets in the solar system, including Earth (but not sun or moon).

> Jupiter, the largest planet, has many moons.

> The goddess of love and a planet are both named Venus.

> There is more water than earth on the planet Earth, so our planet should be named Ocean.

Remember: The third planet from the sun is Earth, a proper noun that should be capitalized. Soil and dirt are earth.

Capitalize historical periods and events.

the Great Depression	the Renaissance
the Middle Ages	the Industrial Revolution
the Revolutionary War	Reconstruction

Capitalize brand names of products.

Nintendo, Tylenol, Nike, Play-Doh, Kodak, Kleenex

Capitalize names of companies, stores, and businesses.

Apple Computer, Inc.	New Balance Athletic Shoe, Inc.
Ford Motor Company	Gap
Procter & Gamble	Starbucks

Capitalize the first word in a direct quotation.

The ringmaster told the crowd, "Elephants, as you can see, are much bigger than pigs."

For more about punctuating direct quotations, see page 97.

Capitalize the first letter of the first word after a colon if it begins a complete sentence.

Remember that old saying: An apple a day keeps the doctor away. (But too many apples can give you indigestion!)

The rule above is actually optional. Some writers capitalize the first word after a colon if it begins a complete sentence, and some don't. However, never capitalize the first word after a colon if it does not begin a full sentence.

Remember to bring all your stuff to the picnic: bug spray, a blanket, the map, and food, food, food!

Colons

Use colons:

- after the greeting in a business letter.

    Dear Sirs: Dear Ms. Freedman: Dear Chairperson:

- to introduce a list.

    You will need the following clothes for the company trip: boots, gloves, a heavy jacket, scarf, and a hat.

- between the hour and the minutes when you use numbers to express time.

    4:34 p.m.   12:52 a.m.

- to introduce a long direct quotation.

    At the press conference, the President declared:

    Times are getting better. The economy is starting to improve, more people are working, crime is down, reading scores are up, the air is getting cleaner, people are buying more homes, factories are humming, and my pet cat just had six adorable kittens.

    Notice that you don't use quotation marks with a long direct quotation. Instead, you indent on both sides from the main text.

Commas

Put a comma:

- before a conjunction that joins the independent clauses in a compound sentence.

    My uncle loves to dance, and my aunt plays the piano.

- after a dependent clause that comes at the beginning of a complex sentence.

  Even though I forgot to study, I still did well on the test.

- between a city and a state.

  Boston, Massachusetts

- between the day and year in a date.

  August 14, 1941

  (Don't put a comma in a date if it's only the month and the year—*August 1941*.)

- to separate three or more words or phrases in a series.

  For my birthday I want a video game, an underwater watch, and a butterfly net.

- after the greeting and closing in a friendly letter.

  Dear Ms. Youngman,   Sincerely yours,

- after introductory words at the beginnings of sentences.

  No, you can't dye your hair green.

- after mild interjections.

  Oh, I didn't know today was the big day.

- to set off the person you're speaking to.

  Lenny, I've been expecting you since Friday.

  I've been expecting you, my tardy friend, since Friday.

- to set off appositives.

  Jen, the craziest kid in our class, scored the most points.

■ with words that interrupt the basic idea of the sentence.

> *Aunt Roslyn, of course, would not wear the parrot costume.*

> *George, therefore, had to leave the drugstore in a hurry.*

■ to separate two adjectives that modify the same noun.

> *The huge, furry dog chased him over the fence and into the pool.*

> **If you're not sure whether or not to put a comma between two adjectives in a row, ask yourself if you can substitute "and" for the comma. "The huge (and) furry dog" gets a comma but not "the spoiled (and) turkey sandwich."**

■ in front of short direct quotations in the middle of a sentence.

> *Then he asked, "How did you get here without a balloon?"*

■ at the end of a direct quotation that is a statement (not a question or an exclamation) when it comes at the beginning of a sentence.

> *"Today must be Tuesday," she muttered.*

Dashes

Use dashes:

■ before and after comments, questions, exclamations, or other interrupters that you write into a sentence to give information or add extra emphasis.

Two rooms—the cafeteria and the library—were flooded.

The mayor—he's my aunt's boyfriend—came to the assembly today.

■ to introduce a list of items.

The teacher said that these were the five most important steps in doing our homework—write it down, take it home, do it, bring it back, hand it in.

> **You can use dashes instead of other punctuation marks like parentheses, commas, or colons to show more emphasis, add information, or create special effects. Don't overdo any one kind of punctuation mark. Use variety in your writing.**

■ after an interrupted or unfinished statement or thought.

I knew it couldn't possibly be Nita, and yet—

Ellipses

Ellipses are three or four dots in a row. Ellipses replace words that have been left out. Use three dots to show that words have been left out in the middle of a passage:

I pledge allegiance to the flag of the United States of America and to the republic for which it stands, One nation . . . with liberty and justice for all.

Use four dots if the words left out come at the end of the sentence:

To be or not to be. . . .

Exclamation Points

Put an exclamation point:

- after strong interjections.

  Oh, no! I lost my mother's earrings!

- after exclamatory sentences.

  I can't stand this place anymore!

- after strong imperative sentences.

  Sit down and be quiet, you nut!

Hyphens

Use a hyphen:

- to break a word between syllables at the end of a line.

  The famous Italian sculptor, painter, and archi-
  tect, Michelangelo, was born in 1475.

- in two-part numbers from twenty-one to ninety-nine written as words.

  twenty-one   *fifty-three*   *sixty-eight*

- in fractions written as words.

  one-third   *two-fifths*   *fifteen-sixteenths*

- in some compound nouns and adjectives

  well-known   *know-it-all*   *drive-in*

Indenting

When you indent, you set the first word of a line in from the left margin.

Indent:

- at the beginning of each new paragraph.

    If you are using a word processor, indent about five spaces from the left margin by hitting the space bar a few times or by hitting the tab key once. Indent about one inch if you are writing your paper by hand.

    > *One of the most famous speeches ever given in the twentieth century is Dr. Martin Luther King, Jr.'s, famous "I Have a Dream" speech. He delivered it on August 28, 1963, standing in front of the Lincoln Memorial in Washington, DC, in front of hundreds of thousands of people at a civil rights rally. The speech was broadcast on television that day, and it has been replayed many times since, most notably on Martin Luther King Day every January.*

    Not all writers indent the first sentence of each new paragraph. Sometimes in business letters and in some books, writers skip a line between paragraphs without indenting. That's another way to show the reader where one paragraph ends and the next one begins. It's your choice, but if you do indent, be consistent. Do it throughout your paper.

- all lines of a long quotation.

    If you are quoting more than four or five lines from a poem or from any other source, indent all the lines ten spaces from the left margin if you are typing or using a word processor. Indent all lines approximately two inches from the left margin if you are writing. Don't use quotation marks if you indent a whole quoted passage.

> *Rain, rain, I hate to complain,*
> *But you are driving me insane;*
> *I thought I had made it perfectly plain,*
> *That I didn't want you here again;*
> *So please abstain, oh rainy rain,*
> *From raining on my windowpane;*
> *Thank you.*

> *At the back of your elbow in your upper arm is a bone called "humerus" in Latin. "Humerus" sounds like "humorous," so many years ago people started calling that bone the "funny bone." If something makes you laugh, people say that it "tickles your funny bone." That is the origin of that famous idiom.*

Italics

Letters that slant to the right are in italics. Most word processing programs on computers allow you to type in italics when you want to.

Use italics:

■ for titles.

magazines:	operas:
The New Yorker	*The Marriage of Figaro*
newspapers:	musical shows:
USA Today	*Fiddler on the Roof*
books:	movies:
Freedom's Children	*Jurassic Park*

plays: television shows:

　　Death of a Salesman　　　*Seinfeld*

　　　radio programs: *All Things Considered*

You can also underline these titles instead of putting them into italics. See the section on underlining on page 103.

■ for stage directions in the script of a play.

> JENNIFER: *(hysterically throwing her plate on the floor)*
> I will never eat meat again! Never! Never!

Stage directions in a script of a play can be printed in italics with or without brackets or parentheses. It depends on who is writing or typing the script.

■ to emphasize a word for special effect.

> *She* asked him to marry her?

> She asked *him* to marry her?

> She asked him to *marry* her?

> She asked him to marry *her*?

Do you see how changing the word in italics changes the feeling the writer is trying to express in each of the sentences above?

Parentheses

Use parentheses:

■ to give the reader extra information.

> *To order the Gut Buster, call our toll-free number (800-GUT-BUST).*

> *For more on short giraffes, read chapter 12 (pages 27–38).*

■ around the abbreviation or acronym of an organization or company after you've written its full name.

> *She worked for the National Aeronautics and Space Administration (NASA).*

■ to put a statement, question, direction, or exclamation, or some other information that's not really part of the sentence, into the sentence. (You do this for extra effect, as in this case.)

> *She got help from Dave (he's a brain) and still flunked the test.*

> **You can use a question mark or an exclamation point—but not a period—at the end of an expression in parentheses when it's in the middle of a sentence.**
>
> *Jen's cousin Cindy (do you know her?) moved back to Chicago.*

Periods

Put a period:

- at the end of a declarative sentence.

  The batteries in my cassette player are dead.

- at the end of an imperative sentence that makes a request, gives an instruction, or states a mild order.

  Always shut off the computer when you're finished.

- after most initials.

  John F. Kennedy

- after most abbreviations.

  P.O. Box 325

  116 Binghamton Ave.

  Mt. Renae, CA

> Do not use a period with the postal service abbreviation of a state. Examples: MA, NY, FL

Question Marks

Put a question mark at the end of a question.

  Why are you doing that disgusting thing?

> Don't use a question mark after a polite request that sounds like a question but really isn't.

  Will you please sign your name here.

Quotation Marks

Always put quotation marks before and after the names of:

■ articles in magazines and newspapers.

> *I cut out "The Amazing Life of a Hummingbird" from Sunday's paper.*

■ chapters in books.

> *Read the chapter called "The Boy from the Clouds" for homework.*

■ essays and short stories.

> *My sister's essay, "How to Improve This School," won the award!*

> *The story "Dark and Stormy Night" was scary, but funny.*

■ songs and poems.

> *For the talent show I'm singing "Dragon, Why Are You Dragging?"*

> *"Love Among Petunias" is in the literary magazine.*

Use quotation marks:

■ to set off words or phrases that are special for any reason.

> *I got "ambidextrous" right on the spelling test.*

> *He explained "the pursuit of happiness" in class yesterday.*

■ before and after a direct quotation (someone's exact words).

Notice that periods, commas, and other punctuation marks that end or interrupt a quotation go inside the second set of quotation marks.

Mary said, "I haven't seen such a mess since the last tornado."

"I haven't seen such a mess since the last tornado," said Mary.

"I haven't seen such a mess," said Mary, "since the last tornado."

"I haven't seen such a mess in ages," said Mary. "The last time was the last tornado."

Do not use quotation marks with an **indirect quotation**, words that do not quote someone exactly:

Mary said that she hadn't seen such a mess since the last tornado.

Direct Quotations

A direct quote (or quotation) repeats the *exact words* a person said or wrote.

There is a difference between direct and indirect quotations.

Direct (use quotation marks):
Harriet told me, "I love living in New York City."

Indirect (do not use quotation marks):
Harriet told me that she loves living in New York City.

Here are twelve good rules about punctuating direct quotations:

1. Put quotation marks around the direct quotation (the exact words that came out of a person's mouth).

   Cindy said, "Take Jade to the store with you, John."

   "Where's Ashley's book?" Dennis asked Lynda. "I can't find it anywhere."

2. Capitalize the first word of a direct quotation.

   Jessica told Aaron, "That's a great haircut you got."

3. If the direct quotation is broken into two parts, don't capitalize the first word of the second part (unless it's a proper noun, a proper adjective, or the pronoun I).

   "Shana, my dear sister," whispered Sasha, "where is my favorite blue skirt?"

4. If the direct quote is broken into two parts, put a comma at the end of the first part (before the first closing quotation mark) and another comma before the second opening quotation mark.

   "Stan, will you wear your chicken costume when you go golfing," asked Helene, "or should I put it in the laundry?"

5. Put a comma before the first quotation mark (when the sentence does not begin with the direct quotation).

   Zach shouted to Zoe from the top-floor window, "Where did you hide the dog?"

6. Put a colon after an independent clause that introduces a quote (especially if the quote is four or more lines

long and is formal, such as in a research paper, official report, or business letter).

> *Bonnie's announcement to the crowd was shocking: "Kurt and I are eloping tonight! Saddle the horses. Cancel the wedding. Notify the press. Stand back. Don't try to talk us out of it. Our minds are made up!"*

7. If the sentence continues after the direct quote, you may end the direct quote with a question mark, an exclamation mark, or a comma, but not a period. Use a comma instead of a period. (A period can come only at the end of a sentence.)

> *She asked, "Is that me?" and started to cry.*

> *She screamed, "That isn't me!" and her face turned scarlet.*

> *She murmured, "That's me," and quickly walked away.*

8. If the direct quote comes at the end of a sentence, the final punctuation mark before the closing quotation mark may be a period, question mark, or exclamation mark, but not a comma.

> *He whispered, "That's my train."*

> *He asked, "When does the train get here?"*

> *He shouted, "I missed my train!"*

9. If the direct quotation is long (with four or more sentences or many words), do not use quotation marks. Use a colon to introduce the quotation. Indent the whole quotation about ten spaces or two inches from the left. Leave two lines blank both before and after the quotation.

My favorite part of the Declaration of Independence says:

> *When, in the Course of human events, it becomes necessary for one people to dissolve the political bands which have connected them with another, and to assume among the powers of the earth, the separate and equal station to which the Laws of Nature and of Nature's God entitle them, a decent respect to the opinions of mankind requires that they should declare the causes which impel them to the separation.*

10. When you quote what someone said or wrote, and it is more than one paragraph long, put opening quotation marks at the beginning of each paragraph. Put closing quotations marks only at the end of the whole quotation, not at the end of each paragraph.

> *The great Native American Chief Hiawatha spoke to the leaders of five Native American nations in the 1500s. He was trying to convince them to stop fighting among themselves and unite. He said:*
>
> *"You, the people sitting in the shade of the great tree whose roots dig deeply into the earth and whose branches spread far and wide, shall be the first nation because you are fearsome and powerful.*
>
> *"And you, the people who rest yourselves against the eternal, immovable stone, shall be the second nation because you always provide wise guidance.*
>
> *"And you, the people who have your home at the foot of the great mountain and are shaded by its projecting rocks, shall be the third nation because you are all highly skilled in speaking."*

The speech worked. The five nations formed the Iroquois Federation.

11. When you quote a conversation between two or more people, start a new paragraph every time a different person starts to speak.

   "Which cat knocked over the vase of flowers," Karen asked, "Tiger or Peaches?"

   Fatima answered, "I think it was Peaches."

   "How can you tell?" asked Franklin.

   "Because," said Fatima, "Tiger is pointing an accusing paw at Peaches. And Peaches looks guilty."

   "Aaarrgh!" growled Peaches as she ran away.

12. Use single quotation marks to enclose a quote within a quote.

   Loraine told me, "I heard the zookeeper say, 'The gorilla has escaped!' but I really didn't believe it until I felt this hairy hand on my shoulder."

Single Quotation Marks

Use only one quotation mark at either end when a quote is written within another quote:

   "Ellen, I still haven't seen your report on 'Malcolm X: By Any Means Necessary,'" said Ms. Baldwin.

Semicolons

Use a semicolon:

- to join the independent clauses of a compound sentence together when you don't use a comma and a conjunction.

    Chorus meets every Tuesday; band rehearsal is on Wednesday.

- in front of some conjunctions that join together two simple sentences into one compound sentence. In these cases, put a semicolon in front of the conjunction and a comma after it.

    I usually like pecan pie; however, today I don't want any.

    She's been absent this week; therefore, she hasn't read the book.

    You've been mean to me all day; nevertheless, I'll still help you.

Other conjunctions and phrases punctuated this way:	
accordingly	*in addition*
also	*indeed*
as a result	*in fact*
besides	*moreover*
consequently	*on the contrary*
for example	*on the other hand*
for instance	*otherwise*
for this reason	*that is*
furthermore	*thus*
hence	*yet*

■ in a series of three or more items when commas are used within the items.

> *Appearing on tonight's show are Brenda, the wonder frog; Tulip, the talking toucan; and Henrietta, the hip hippo.*

Underlining

In handwritten or typed work, underline the names of:

■ books, magazines, and newspapers.

> *Did you read My Teacher Is from Mars?*

> *I have a subscription to Bullfrogs and Toads magazine.*

> *Her picture is in the Daily Herald-Gazette today.*

■ movies, plays, musicals, operas, and television shows.

> *I never go to horror movies like Flying Snakes Eat Cleveland.*

> *Last night we saw Tosca at the opera house.*

> *For graduation my class is putting on Abe Lincoln in the White House.*

> *Fearless Fred, my favorite show, is on Channel 6 tonight!*

In books or other printed works, the names of books, movies, magazines, etc., are often printed in italics instead of being underlined. When words are italicized, the letters slant.

> *There's a review of The Secrets of the Aardvark in today's Tribune.*

Part 3
Spelling

A Dozen and One Spelling Rules

Here are some helpful rules:

Adding Suffixes

1. Don't change the spelling of the root word when you add the suffix **ly** to any word that doesn't end in **y**.

   Examples:
   sincere + ly = sincerely
   beautiful + ly = beautifully

   Exceptions:
   true + ly = truly
   whole + ly = wholly

2. Don't change the spelling of the root word when you add the suffix **ness** to any word that does not end in the letter **y**.

   Examples:
   kind + ness = kindness
   rough + ness = roughness

3. Keep the silent **e** at the end of a word when you add a suffix that begins with a **consonant** (like **m**ent, **f**ul, and **ly**).

   Examples:
   arrange + ment = arrangement
   peace + ful = peaceful
   sincere + ly = sincerely

Exceptions:
acknowledge + ment = acknowled**gm**ent
judge + ment = jud**gm**ent
true + ly = tru**ly**
whole + ly = who**ll**y

4. Drop the silent **e** at the end of a word when you add a suffix that begins with a **vowel** (such as **ed**, **ing**, **ous**, **ably**, **al**, and **y**).

Examples:
hope + ing = ho**p**ing
shine + y = shi**n**y
fortune + ate = fortu**n**ate
dose + age = do**s**age
nature + al = natu**r**al
fame + ous = fa**m**ous

Exceptions: notic**e**able and courag**e**ous

5. Double the final consonant when the word is just one syllable, the last two letters are **one vowel + one consonant**, and you add a suffix that begins with a vowel (such as ing, ed, er, est, al, y, etc.).

Examples:
swim, swi**mm**ing, swi**mm**er
drag, dra**gg**ing, dra**gg**ed
hot, ho**tt**er, ho**tt**est
rob, ro**bb**ing, ro**bb**er
flop, flo**pp**y, flo**pp**ing

6. Change the **y** to **i** before adding the suffix when you add the suffixes **ness**, **age**, or **ly** to any word that ends in the letter **y**.

Examples:
busy + ness = business
lonely + ness = loneliness
marry + age = marriage
happy + ness = happiness
day + ly = daily

7. Add **ful**, not **full**, when you add the suffix **ful** to any word.

    Examples:
    thought + ful = thoughtful
    cheer + ful = cheerful

Forming Plurals

8. Just add **s** when a word ends with **o** and there's a **vowel** before the o.

    Examples:
    one rodeo, two rodeos
    one radio, two radios

9. Add **es** when a word ends with **o** and there's a **con-sonant** before the o.

    Examples:
    one tomato, two tomatoes
    one torpedo, two torpedoes

    Exception: With words that end with **o** and have something to do with **music**, just add **s** to form their **plurals:**
    alto, altos
    solo, solos
    piano, pianos

Note: With the following words, either plural is correct, but the first is preferred: tornados or tornadoes, mosquitos or mosquitoes, dominos or dominoes, halos or haloes, mottos or mottoes, zeros or zeroes.

10. Just add **s** when the word ends with the letter **y** and there is a **vowel** before the **y**.

   Examples:
   one boy, two boys
   one key, two keys

11. Change the **y** to **i** and add **es** when the word ends with the letter **y**, and there is a **consonant** before the **y**.

   Examples:
   one lady, two ladies
   one country, two countries

Forming Compounds

12. Don't change the spelling of either word when you want to put **two words together** to form a new compound word.

   Examples:
   baby + sitter = baby-sitter
   teen + age = teenage
   shoe + lace = shoelace

   If the first word ends with the same letter that the second word begins with, keep both letters in the middle of the new compound word.

   Examples:
   room + mate = roommate

night + time = nighttime

Exception: past + time = pastime

Note: Sometimes the compound word will be one word (example: **sandpaper**), two words (example: **high school**), or a word with a hyphen in the middle (example: **custom-made**).

There's no rule for this. If you're not sure which version of your compound word is correct, look it up.

An Old Rhyme

13.   **I** before **e** (or is it **e** before **i**?)

If you know a word has the letters **i** and **e** in it together, but you can't remember which comes first, recite this well-known poem:

I *before* **e**
Except after **c**
Or when sounded like **a**
As in neighbor *and* weigh

That rule will work for most words such as: **achievement, believe, brief, chief, die, grief, lie, pie, retrieve, tie, unwieldy, ceiling, conceit, conceited, conceive, deceit, deceive, perceive, receipt, receive, beige, eighty, freight, neigh, reign, reindeer, sleigh, veil, vein, weight.**

Exceptions: Here are some words that do the *opposite* of the poem: **ancient, being, caffeine, codeine, counterfeit, deficient, efficient, either, financier, foreign, forfeit, heifer, height, heir, kaleidoscope, leisure, neither, protein, scientist, seismologist,**

seize, sheik, sleight, society, species, stein, sufficient, their, weird.

Memory Tricks

Trying to spell some words can be very difficult. Sometimes it helps to know a trick or two. Here are some good
memory tricks for more than 150 words that are often
spelled wrong:

accident
car crash + **dent** = accident.

accommodations
At the **c**lean, **c**ute, **m**arvelous **m**otel, the accommodations are good.

acre
The cathedral is built on a **sacred acre** of land.

address
ad + dress = address

advice
My ad**vice** is don't slip on the **ice**.

advise
I ad**vise** you not to catch your finger in the **vise**.

all right
All right is all wrong if it's not *two words*.

altar
The workman got **tar** on the church al**tar**.

alter
She had to al**ter** the **ter**rible gown.

altogether
The **alto** sings **altogether** lovely songs.

amateur
I, an **amateur, am at Eur**ope's shores.

answer
Were you going to give the an**swer**?

architect
The **archi**tect drew the **arch**.

arctic
The first **c** in ar**c**tic stands for **c**old.

arithmetic
I **met** my arith**met**ic teacher at the mall.

athlete
In the b**ath let** e**very athlete** soak tired muscles.

attendance
at + ten + dance = attendance

autumn
There are **m**any **n**ice events at the end of autu**mn**.

awful
Alligator **w**as **f**eeling **u**nhappy **l**ately. How **awful**!

baggage
Ba**ggage** is lu**ggage**.

balloon
A **ball**oon can be shaped like a **ball**.

banana
This **b**an**ana** is *triple-A* quality.

bargain
You can **gain** a lot if you get a bar**gain**.

bazaar
You can **b**uy **a**ncient **z**ebras and **a**musing **r**abbits at a **bazaar**.

beautiful
My **beau** (boyfriend) called me **beau**tiful.

beggar
Did the **beggar beg** in front of the **gar**age?

beginning
The second **inning** is beg**inning**.

behavior
To hit someone with your **vio**lin is bad beha**vior**.

believe
Don't bel**ie**ve a **lie**.

bicycle
It's dangerous to ride a **bicycle** on an **icy** road.

bookkeeper
This is the only word with three sets of double letters in a row: **oo kk ee**.

brake
For goodness's **sake**, step on the br**ake**!

break
"**Brea**k **brea**d" means to eat.

buoy
This **buo**y warns ships of **u**nderwater obstacles.

burglar
A bur**glar** doesn't like the **glar**e of a light.

business
bus + in + ess = business

capital
A is the first capit**al** letter of the **al**phabet.

capitol
The dome on the capitol building is round like the **o** in capit**o**l.

captain
On your **cap** there is a s**tain**, **captain**.

cemetery
Do you scream "e . . . e . . . e!"
when you go past a **cemetery**?

cereal
This ce**real** is made of **real** oats.

chief
"**Hi**," said the c**hi**ef.

chocolate
I was **late**, so I ate all the choco**late**.

choose
Why did the m**oose** ch**oose** a g**oose** with l**oose** feathers?

college
There's a **leg** in col**leg**e.

colonel
The **lone** co**lone**l won the battle.

committee
Marvelous Mike, Terrific Tom, and Elegant Eve are on
the co**mm**ittee.

compliment
I am grateful for your nice compliment.

Connecticut
Connect me to **Connect**icut, please.

conscience
In **science** class, we are studying a frog's con**scie**nce.

corps
P.S. The last two letters in cor**ps** are silent.

correspondence
In his **den,** he read his correspon**den**ce.

criticize
Don't criti**ciz**e the pri**z**e.

dessert
I like something **s**weet for de**ss**ert.

doctor
If you follow the doctor's orders, you'll get well.

dyeing
Don't leave the **dye in** too long when you're **dyeing**
your hair.

eighth
Eighth begins with **eight**.

exaggerate
Good g**r**ief! There's a **rat** in exagge**rat**e!

existence
There **is** a **ten** in exis**ten**ce.

extraordinary
This is more than ordinary. It's **extra**ordinary.

February
Cold people say "**br**" in Fe**br**uary.

fiend
Let's put an **end** to this fi**end**.

flammable
Many **m**atches are fla**mm**able.

foreign
The **foreign** man needed a room **for eig**ht nights.

forth
March **fort**h from the **fort**.

forty
The **fort** held out for **fort**y days.

fourth
Four is the **four**th number.

gallon
All I need is a ga**ll**on.

gnarled
Gee, this is a **nar**row **led**ge to climb with **gnarled** hands.
(Note: The "g" in **gnarled** is silent.)

governor
The **governor** will **govern or** we won't vote for him.

grammar
Don't **mar** (spoil) your writing with bad gram**mar**.

guarantee
The **guar**d, **an** old friend, will **tee** off at three o'clock.

hangar
A han**gar** is like a **gar**age for planes.

hanger
Do you feel **anger** when your clothes fall off your h**anger**?

hear
With my **ear** I h**ear**.

here, there, where
All three words end with "**ere**."

immigrant
Many **m**illions of people were **grant**ed the right to be i**mmigrant**s.

inoculation
An **in**oculation is when the doctor sticks the needle **in**.

interrupt
It's really rude to interrupt someone.

it's
If you can substitute "**it is**," then it's "**it's**."

language
This lang**uage** has been spoken since a long-ago **age**.

library
It's **rar**e not to find a good book in the lib**rar**y.

license
Do **lice** have a **lice**nse to live here?

loose, noose, goose
Take the **noose** off the neck of the **loose goose**.

lose
Did the clown **lose** his rubber **nose**?

maintenance
The **main** thing is for **ten** of the **mainten**ance men to
    fix the leak.

mantel
Can the **man tele**phone from the **mantel**?

marriage
If I **marry**, will **I age** faster after my **marriage**?

mathematics
Ma, the mat has **mathemat**ics written on it.

medieval
Did many people **die** in medieval times?

mileage
mile + age = mileage

miscellaneous
In his **cell**, the prisoner found mis**cell**aneous things.

misspell
Miss Pell would **misspell** everything!

naive
An**na, I've** been so **naive**.

niece
This **piece** belongs to my n**iece**.

occasion

This special occasion calls for coconut custard and
soda.

occur

When did the car crash occur?

often

She gives the right answer nine out **of ten** times, which
is pretty **often**.

ough words

I'm tough and thorough, and I fought through the
rough storm, and I thought I had sought and
bought and brought enough cough syrup for the
whole winter.

pageant

page + ant = pageant

pajamas

Did **Pa jam** his **pajam**as in the drawer?

parallel

The two **l**'s in parallel are parallel lines.

pavilion

There's a **lion** in the pavilion!

peace

There's peace in this place.

physician

What is the **physician**'s **ph**one number?

piece

Please cut me a **piece** of **pie**.

playwright
The playwright wrote a beautiful play.

porpoise
Is that noise coming from the porpoise?

potatoes
Her toes looked like little potatoes.

prairie
The air on the prairie is fresh and clean.

prey
Predators prey on other animals.

principal
The principal of the school is your pal.

principle
A principle is a rule of life.

professor
A professor is frequently someone smart.

pronunciation
The nun has clear pronunciation.

purchase
She opened her purse to make her purchase.

quiet
Try a quiet diet.

quite
You have quite an appetite.

raspberry
Grasp the raspberry and squeeze it.

realize
I **realiz**ed the diamond was **real**.

receipt
Shh! The **p** is silent in receipt.

recipe
The **recipe** calls for **ripe** vegetables.

resistance
Sis has a **tan** in re**sistan**ce.

restaurant
Rest, dino**saur** and **ant**, at this **restaurant**.

rhinoceros
The **rh**inoceros writes **rh**ymes.

ridiculous
He had to get **rid** of his **rid**iculous hat.

role
He has a **role** in the **whole** play.

roll
I tried to **roll** the tr**oll** over the kn**oll**.

safety
Be **safe**. Practice **safe**ty.

scene
I was **sc**ared by that **sc**ene in the movie.

scheme
He hatched a **sch**eme to get out of **sch**ool.

scissors
With **sc**issors, he cut the hair off his **sc**alp.

secretary
The **secret**ary has a **secret** she's not telling. There's **tar** on the secre**tar**y's shoes.

separate
There's **a rat** in sep**arat**e.

shriek
"**Die**!" he shr**ie**ked.

skiing
Keep both your **i**'s open when sk**ii**ng.

soldier
The sol**dier** did not **die**.

squeak
Does the mouse sp**eak** with a squ**eak**?

stationary
The **a** in station**a**ry stands for st**a**y.

stationery
The **e** in station**e**ry stands for **e**nvelope.

steal
Did he st**eal** the **real** treasure?

steel
The wh**eel** is made of st**eel**.

surgeon
I will **urge on** the s**urge on** to perform the operation.

sword
Take my **word** for it, this s**word** is sharp.

than
I like this **plan** better than Dan's **plan**.

their, there, they're
All three begin with **"the."**

thief
A thief will **lie**.

tomorrow
Tom, there will be no **sorrow tomorrow**.

tongue
An elephant's **tongue** weighs a **ton**, and he uses it to ar**gue**.

tragedy
Old **age** is not a tragedy.

trouble
This is not **our** trouble; it's y**our** trouble.

vacuum
Make sure to vacuum **up u**nder the sofa.

villain
The **villain** lives in a **villa in** the country.

weather
In rainy **weather, we** look **at her** picture.

Wednesday
She will **wed** next **Wed**nesday.

which
Whi**ch rich** person donated the money?

witch
The w**itch** scratched her **itch**.

yacht
This is the **ba**chelor's **yacht**.

yolk
The gentle **folk** eat the **yolk**.

Part 4
Letter Writing

Friendly Letters

Five (Really Six) Parts of a Friendly Letter

1. Heading

The **heading** gives the month, day, and year, and sometimes the day of the week you wrote the letter. The date is important in case it is delayed in the mail or the person refers to your letter when writing back. If the person you are writing to doesn't know your address, include that above the date.

34 Warwick Avenue
Stratford, CT 06497
September 15, 2000

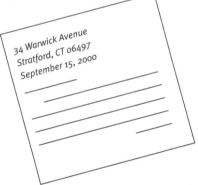

The heading appears in the top right or left corner of the page. Note that the state is not written out, but is abbreviated according to the system used by the U.S. postal service.

2. Salutation

Salutation is a big word for the greeting of your letter. The most traditional and popular salutation for a friendly letter is **Dear** followed by whatever you call that person (Charlie, Uncle George, Grandma, Dr. Green, etc.). The salutation appears on the left side of the page below the heading. The person's name is followed by a comma.

Dear Lucy,

Dear Uncle Bob,

Dear Dr. Lewis,

Dear Uncle Bob,

3. Body

The body is the main part of the letter where you write what you have to say to the person. It can be one or several paragraphs, and it should have a beginning, a middle, and an end. Start with a greeting, then tell your news, and end with a good-bye. If your letter deals with more than one subject or topic, you should begin each subject with a new indented paragraph.

What's new with you? Mom says you are coming to visit next month. Could you bring me the photos from your trip to the dude ranch? I want to use them for a report in school.
Thanks a lot. Can't wait to see you.

4. *Closing*

The closing is the ending to your letter. Unlike the salutation, there are many closings to choose from. Here are some of the more popular ones: **Sincerely, Your friend, Love, All the best.** Choose the closing that is most appropriate to the person to whom you are writing. For example, if the person is a close friend or relative, **Love** is a fitting closing. With an acquaintance, you might close with **Sincerely** or **All the best.**

Sincerely,

Your friend,

Love,

All the best,

Love,

5. Signature

The **signature** is especially important because it identifies the letter writer. It should appear directly under the closing. If you are sure the person will know who you are, just sign your first name. If not, add your last name.

   A signature is your personal mark, like your fingerprint. It should always be written by hand, even if the rest of the letter is written on a computer or typewriter. Make sure your signature is legible so your correspondent can read it.

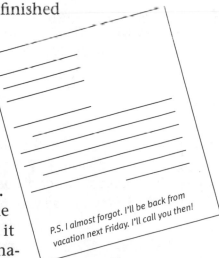

Hindy Smallwood
Andra Vebell
Ralph Lamar

6. P.S. (Postscript)

Sometimes when you're finished writing a letter, you remember something else you wanted to say. To avoid having to write the entire letter over again, you can add a postscript. Postscript comes from Latin and means **after writing**. It is a brief addition to the body of your letter, and it appears below the signa-

P.S. I almost forgot. I'll be back from vacation next Friday. I'll call you then!

ture. It is always prefaced by the abbreviation **P.S.** Note the word *brief*. If a postscript is too long, you might as well write another letter.

Read Your Letter Again!

When you're finished, read your letter over. Take the time to check your spelling, grammar, and punctuation. Make any necessary corrections right on the letter. However, if this gets too messy, copy your letter again. You want the person to whom you're writing to be able to read it.

Here is a friendly letter:

Heading	*34 Warwick Avenue* *Stratford, CT 06497* *September 15, 2000*
Salutation	*Dear Uncle Bob,*
Body	*What's new with you?* *Mom says you are coming to visit next month. Could you bring me the photos from your trip to the dude ranch? I want to use them for a report in school. Thanks a lot.* *Can't wait to see you.*
Closing	*Love,*
Signature	*Tom*
Postscript	*P.S. I almost forgot. I'll be back from vacation next Friday. I'll call you then!*

Thank-you Notes, Invitations, and Announcements

Thank-you Notes

There are two main kinds of thank you notes—a thank-you note for a gift and a thank-you note for a visit.

A Thank-you Note for a Gift You Like

Thank-you notes let people know that you received their gift and appreciate their thoughtfulness.

Here are some things to keep in mind when writing a thank-you note for a gift:

■ **Be prompt.** The note should be written within a week or two of receiving the gift.

■ **Be specific.** Maybe it's your birthday and you got many gifts. Mention the gift by name, so the person knows that you know which gift he or she gave you.

■ **Explain how you will use/are using the gift.** This shows the gift is something you really need and appreciate.

Here are a couple of thank-you notes for gifts:

January 7, 2000

Dear Grandma,

Name gifts specifically

    I really love the videotapes you sent for Christmas. <u>Star Wars</u> is one of my all-time favorite movies, and I really like <u>Toy Story</u>, too. I've already watched them three times each!
    Thanks for the movies. Have a happy new year.

Love,

Lauren

July 25, 2000

Dear Mr. Cooper,

How you will use the gift

    How did you know I wanted a basketball for my birthday? I played with it yesterday with some of my friends, and I got four baskets.
    Thanks a lot. Now you have to come and see me play basketball this summer.

Sincerely,

Joey Morella

A Thank-you Note for a Gift You Don't Like

This is a delicate situation that requires some thought. You don't want to hurt the person's feelings. Here are some pointers:

- **Avoid insincerity.** Don't say you love the gift when you really don't. It's better to say very little than to lie.

- **Focus on the person.** Whether you like the gift or not, it shows the person's thoughtfulness. Thank the giver for thinking of you.

Here are two thank-you notes for gifts you don't like:

Focus on the person

> August 15, 2000
>
> Dear Uncle George,
>
>   Thank you for the book on trees. It was very nice of you to remember my graduation.
>   My party was great. Everyone had fun. I'm sorry you couldn't be there. Hope you come visit us this summer.
>   Take care.
>
> Your niece,
>
> Kris

January 7, 2000

Dear Mrs. Rosenfeld,

Thank you for the pen-and-pencil set for my Bar Mitzvah. I feel like a grown-up person now, except that I still have to go to school.
Jessica's Bat Mitzvah is next month. Get ready for another party!

Yours truly,

Ronald Borgen

A Thank-you Note for a Gift of Money

Here are some pointers for writing a thank-you note for a gift of money:

- **Don't mention the amount given.** It's impolite to refer to the exact amount of money. There's also a chance you might mention the wrong amount and confuse the person. Simply refer to it as the "gift of money."

- **Tell what you plan to do with the money.** Let the person know what you're going to spend the money on or what you're saving it for. They'll appreciate knowing it's being put to good use.

Here are two thank-you notes for gifts of money:

Plan for spending the money

> March 14, 2000
>
> Dear Granddad,
>
> Thanks for the money for my birthday. I'm going to use it to save up for a new bicycle. I should be able to buy it real soon. It's red, looks radical, and rides great. Maybe you can come ride with me soon.
>
> Love,
>
> Arnold

How you used the money

> October 12, 2000
>
> Dear Mr. Allen,
>
> I got the check you sent for my birthday. Thank you for the money. I bought a baseball card album with it. I really needed it because I have about a zillion baseball cards that were all over the place. Now I won't ever lose them. Thanks again.
>
> Sincerely,
>
> Robbie Fisher

A Thank-you Note for a Visit

It is polite to write a thank-you note to friends or relatives after you stayed with them. Here are some things to keep in mind:

- **Don't put it off.** Write your thank-you note within a week after your visit.

- **Mention something that you really enjoyed.** This will make your thank-you note more meaningful and sincere.

- **Extend your own invitation.** Let your friend know he or she is welcome to stay with you, too.

Here is a thank-you note after a visit:

<table>
<tr><td></td><td>May 9, 2000</td></tr>
<tr><td></td><td>Dear Sheila:</td></tr>
<tr><td>Something you did</td><td>Thanks for having me over last weekend. Picking blueberries in the woods behind your house was great! The blueberries tasted better than the ones we buy in the city. And I loved your mom's blueberry pancakes.</td></tr>
<tr><td>Thank household</td><td>Please thank her and your dad. And thank your brother Dave for giving up his bed to me. You have a great family.</td></tr>
<tr><td>Invitation</td><td>Now it's your turn to visit me! You can sleep on the top bunk in my room. (Sally won't mind.) Call soon. How about next weekend?</td></tr>
<tr><td></td><td>Your friend,</td></tr>
<tr><td></td><td>Tanya</td></tr>
</table>

Invitations

There are basically two kinds of invitations—invitations to a party and invitations to visit.

Inviting People to a Party

Here are some examples of parties that could require a written invitation:

- birthday parties
- graduation parties
- holiday parties
- club or group get-togethers
- housewarmings

Information to include

You can buy printed invitations at stationery stores, you can make invitations, or you can write a letter. In all cases, make sure to include the following information:

- the type of social occasion
- the date, time, and place of the event (you may want to include written directions or a map)
- information on what to bring or wear
- request for a response to the invitation

Asking for a response

Asking for a response to the invitation helps you to plan how much food, drinks, party favors, and space you will need. A request for a response is usually written in the lower left corner of the invitation and can take two forms:

RSVP These initials stand for the French words *répondez s'il vous plaît,* which means "please reply." Invited guests should reply by phone (if you include your phone number) or they can send a note to tell if they can come or not.

Regrets Only. These words tell people to respond only if they can't attend. Otherwise, you will assume they are coming.

> **An invitation should be mailed at least two weeks before the occasion to give people plenty of time to fit it into their schedules.**

Here is an invitation to a birthday party:

> *November 10, 2000*
>
> *Dear Charles,*
>
> *I'd like to invite you to my 10th birthday party at my house on Saturday, November 27, at 2 p.m. (Check out the map I included with directions to get here.) We're going to be playing games outside, so don't dress up.*
> *I hope you can make it!*
>
> *Your friend,*
>
> *Hank*
>
> *RSVP 677-8130*

Announcements

Announcements tell people when an event or meeting is taking place. They can be posters or flyers that you hang in noticeable spots (like the bulletin board at school), or you can send the information in a letter. Here are some occasions when you would send an announcement:

- a meeting of an after-school group

- a sports event

- a club party or awards celebration

Information to Include

An announcement should be short and to the point. Here are some of the kinds of information it should contain:

- the group that is meeting

- the purpose of the meeting or event

- the date, time, and place the meeting or event will be held

- the phone number and person to call if someone can't attend

- the admission fee or requirements (dress up, bring food), if applicable

Here is an announcement for a meeting in letter form:

March 22, 2000

Dear Karen,

   This is to let you know that the staff of _The Addison Advocate_, our school paper, will be meeting on Monday, March 29 at 3:30 p.m. after school in the _Advocate_ office. We will be planning our next issue. If you can't make it, please call Frank Bronski at 378-2435.
   Hope to see you Monday.

Yours,

Pam Elliot

Editor

Pam gave her full name and title. This kind of announcement is almost like a business letter.

Business Letters

Three Business Letter Formats

- **The block format.** In this format all parts of the letter run along the left side of the page (margin). No paragraphs in the body are indented, but an extra space is left between paragraphs.

- **The modified block format.** In this format the heading and the closing and signature run along the right margin. All the other parts run along the left margin.

- **The semiblock format.** This format is the same as the block format, except that the paragraphs in the body are indented.

In the sample letters in this chapter, we will use the block format.

Six Parts of a Business Letter

1. Heading

The heading consists of your address and the date.

502 Elm Street
Topeka, KS 66608
January 24, 2000

The heading appears about an inch from the top of the page in the top right or left corner, depending on the letter format used.

2. Inside Address

The inside address consists of the name and address of the person to whom you are writing. It usually appears four lines below the heading, and it is always at the left margin.

> Here are some tips for writing the inside address:
>
> ■ It is up to you whether or not you include Mr., Ms., Dr., etc. before the name. However, if the person holds a high public office, such as U.S. Senator or Representative, the words **The Most Honorable** must precede his or her name. Christian religious figures are often addressed with a "the" in an address. For example, **The Reverend.**
>
> ■ If the person has a title (Vice President, Editor), it should be included after the name, either on the same line (separated by a comma) or on the next line.

- If the letter is being sent to the person's workplace, the name of the company or business should be included on a separate line.

Philip Grabowski, Program Director
The Kid Channel
1409 Colonial Blvd.
Philadelphia, PA 19056

3. Salutation

The most traditional salutation, or greeting, for a business letter is **Dear** followed by the word **Mr., Ms., Mrs.,** or **Miss.** This is followed by the person's last name and a colon. All the words in a salutation should begin with capital letters.

Dear Ms. Jones:

Dear Mrs. Lowe:

If you are writing to a company rather than a specific person or position, use one of these other salutations:

To Whom It May Concern:

Dear Sir or Madam:

Dear Ladies and Gentlemen:

Special salutations

Here are some special salutations for professional people or elected officials:

for a religious leader	→	**Dear Rabbi Cohen** (**The Reverend Matthew Jamison** becomes **Dear Mr. Jamison** or **Father Jamison**)
for a college professor	→	**Dear Professor Cook**
for a medical doctor	→	**Dear Dr. Sharp**
for a U.S. Representative	→	**Dear Ms. Ricci**
for a U.S. Senator	→	**Dear Senator Goldfarb**
for the President of the United States	→	**Dear Mr. President** or **Dear President Clinton**

Notice that **Professor, Senator, President, Father,** and **Rabbi** are spelled out in full.

4. Body

The body is the main part of the letter where you write what you have to say to the person. Skip one line after the salutation, and begin. Generally, begin the body of a business letter with a brief personal greeting, then state your business, and end with a thank-you (if necessary).

- **Get to the point.** After a brief greeting, get down to business. Don't waste time in small talk.

- **Don't use slang, and try to avoid contractions.** Business letters are usually formal. Increase your chances of making a good impression by using standard English.

■ **Even though it's a business letter, don't be too formal.** You still want to sound like you.

5. Closing

The closing is the ending to your letter. In the block format, the closing appears in the bottom left corner of the letter, directly under the body.

Only the first word in a closing should be capitalized. It is always followed by a comma. Here are some typical closings:

■ **Truly yours** and **Yours truly** are the most common closings in a business letter.

■ **Sincerely** and **Sincerely yours** are less formal and better to use if you know the person.

■ **Respectfully yours** is used only for important officials.

6. Signature

The signature is your full name, signed. Your signature should appear directly below the closing. It should always be written in ink. Below it, write your name in block letters (or type it four lines below the closing, if you're using a typewriter or computer). This way, if the reader can't read your signature, he or she will still be able to read your name.

Offering a Suggestion

Maybe you want to suggest a way to improve a product (or suggest adding a ride to an amusement park, or improving service at your local restaurant).

Here is a letter that makes a suggestion:

3533 McNair Way
Lexington, KY 40513
September 7, 2000

Poppo's Pizza
238 Sitwell Place
San Francisco, CA 94179

To Whom It May Concern:

Positive response to product, followed by a suggestion

Your frozen pizza really hits the spot, but there aren't enough pieces. Instead of four pieces in each pizza, why not eight? You could make your pizza a little bigger and make each slice smaller. All the kids would think you are a super-nice company.

I hope you will consider my suggestion.

Truly yours,

Daniel Otfinoski

Daniel Otfinoski

The company may not act on your suggestion, but you'll probably get a nice reply. You might get something more. As a thank-you, the boy who wrote the letter above got some discount coupons to buy more pizza.

Writing to School and Public Officials

You might write a letter to a person of authority in school or government to make a complaint, suggestion, or request.

Here is a letter to a school principal that contains both a complaint and a request:

	864 Hillcrest Drive Staunton, VA 24401 April 4, 2000
	Ms. Sherwood, Principal Staunton Elementary Schools 719 Woodwell Road Staunton, VA 24401
	Dear Ms. Sherwood:
States situation	I am writing to you to discuss how Mrs. Ortega has to walk us up to our lockers after school and then outside to the bus line. I think this is unfair. Other sixth graders leave without their
Complaint and reason	teachers. We are no more noisy or misbehaved than any other sixth graders.
Request	If you would give us just one week to try going to our lockers by ourselves, I'm sure our entire class would appreciate it.
Thank-you	Thank you for reading this letter, and I hope you seriously consider my request.
	Sincerely, *Jonathan Warner* Jonathan Warner

Here is a letter of opinion to a public official (in this case the 42nd President of the United States, William J. Clinton, just before his inauguration):

143 Morgan Street
Grover City, CA 93433
January 11, 1993

President William J. Clinton
1600 Pennsylvania Avenue, N.W.
Washington, D.C. 20001

Dear President-elect Clinton:

I am very happy that you will be our President. I'm excited, and I want to hear some of your ideas on making this country better. I would like to suggest three issues that I think you should consider:

Points are specific

1. Economy—Our economy is falling apart, and we need to improve it in order to make progress.

2. Health care—America should spend more money on health care so all people can be healthy and enjoy life.

3. Environment—The natural resources we get from our environment are very special. We need most of them in order to survive. We can't throw them away.

Thank you for your time.

Sincerely,

Toby Anekwe

Toby Anekwe

Letters to the Editor

Most newspapers and magazines have a page or section devoted to letters from readers. These letters are addressed to the editor and are written for a variety of reasons:

- to express an opinion

- to react to another letter, news article, or editorial

- to compliment a person in the community

- to complain about a problem in the community

Whatever kind of letter to the editor you are writing, here are some things to keep in mind as you write:

- **State your opinion clearly.** Be up front about how you feel. The paper or magazine is giving you an opportunity to say what's on your mind. Don't waste it.

- **Provide reasons for your opinion.** The more convincing your argument, the more people will take your opinion seriously.

- **If you are reacting to another article or letter, identify it.** People won't know what you're reacting to if you don't clearly name it and briefly explain what it says.

- **Be polite.** You can be forceful and direct and still be respectful.

Here is a letter to the editor of a local newspaper:

70 Turkey Hill Road
Fort Worth, TX 76156
February 3, 2000

Editor
Fort Worth Star-Telegram
Fort Worth, TX 76156

Dear Editor:

Opinion
stated

Reasons for
opinion

I believe there should be no homework in the city of Fort Worth. Do we not have school six hours a day, thirty hours a week, one hundred twenty hours a month? I believe we get enough work in school, never mind at home. Our teachers believe we are very hard workers. Imagine, homework on top of sports, on top of after-school activities! We want a break.

Sincerely,

Gregory Trupp

Gregory Trupp

Here is a letter to the editor of a news magazine:

24 Hawthorne Drive
Salem, MA 01970
December 10, 2000

Editor
Newsweek Magazine
657 Madison Avenue
New York, NY 10010

Name article

Dear Editor:

Opinion

I don't agree with your November 7 story, "It's
the Breakdown of American Families That Is the
Primary Cause of Children's Problems." I think
the school is at fault, too. If the teachers were
more inspiring, the kids would stay off the
streets. The schools should at least try to keep
them in school.

Further
explanation
of opinion

The family is partly at fault, though. They
should set limits for their kids, so they don't
hang out with dropouts. If they do, their kids
might drop out, too. They might even hang out
with gangs that do drugs.

You can blame both the family and the school.
They both need to take care of the child equally.

Sincerely,

Jay Bertini

Jay Bertini

Addressing the Envelope

Three Parts of an Addressed Envelope

1. Return Address

The **return address** is the name and address of the person sending the letter. It is called the "return address" because if the letter can't be delivered, for whatever reason, it will be returned to that address. If you forgot to include the return address, an undelivered letter will end up at a place called the "dead-letter office."

The return address usually appears in the top left corner of the envelope and consists of your name, street address, city or town, state, and zip code.

On some personal correspondence, the return address can appear on the sealed flap of the opposite side of the envelope.

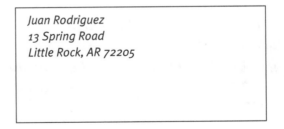

Juan Rodriguez
13 Spring Road
Little Rock, AR 72205

2. Mailing Address

The **mailing address** is the name and address to which the letter is being sent. It always appears in the center of the envelope.

In a **personal letter,** the address consists of a name, street address, city or town, state, and zip code. Include an apartment number, if needed.

In a **business letter**, the address on the envelope is the same as the inside address of the letter. There may be separate lines for the title of the addressee (President, Editor, etc.), the division or department the person works in, and the name of his or her company, business, or organization.

Jane Cardwell
President
Quick-Rite Computer Software, Inc.
668 Ripley Boulevard
Los Angeles, CA 21021

If the name of the company or organization is very long, you might want to continue it on a second line, slightly indented.

Quick-Rite Computer
*   Software, Inc.*

Sometimes you will be asked to write a business letter to a department at a business or organization, but you want it to go to a particular person, if possible. Write the word "Attention" followed by a colon and the person's name in the lower left corner of the envelope.

Juan Rodriguez
13 Spring Road
Little Rock, AR 72205

Circulation Department
The Connecticut Post
P.O. Box 1055
Trumbull, CT 06611

Attention: Cal Smith

3. *Postage*

A letter will not be delivered without a stamp. The stamp should always be attached in the upper right corner of the envelope. The amount of the stamp depends on the kind of mail you are sending (letter, postcard, package), how fast you want it to get there, and how much it weighs. Ask your family, teacher, or the post office for the correct postage.

Envelope sizes

Business letters should be mailed in standard business envelopes, which are rectangular and measure 4 inches by 9½ inches. Personal letters can be sent in any size envelope. The smallest envelope the Postal Service will accept is 3½ inches by 5 inches. A letter, especially a business letter, should be folded neatly in thirds, from the bottom up and the top down, before being sealed in an envelope.

Tips for Addressing an Envelope

- **Always write the address in ink or on a typewriter.** Never use pencil to write an address. It can be erased or may come off if it gets wet.

- **Write legibly.** If your handwriting is not completely clear, write the address in block letters or type it. If the mail carrier can't read the address, it will come back to you or end up in the dead-letter office.

Here is an addressed envelope for a business letter:

> Martha Jackson
> 570 Palm Drive
> Fort Lauderdale, FL 33329
>
> Editor, *Junior Scholastic*
> Scholastic Inc.
> 555 Broadway
> New York, NY 10012

Addressing Mail to a Person Outside the United States

Any letter being mailed outside the United States requires the name of the country on both the return address and the mailing address. It will require more postage. Remember to write "AIR MAIL" on it to remind the post office.

Here is an envelope addressed to a person outside the United States:

> Alex O'Neill
> 12 Otter Way
> Montpelier, VT 05602
> USA
>
> Susan Moore   AIR MAIL
> 13 Reginald Lane
> Milton of Campsie
> Glasgow G65 8EQ
> Scotland

If you write regularly to a pen pal or friend over-seas, you might want to buy some aerogrammes. These lightweight combination stationery/envelopes cost less to mail than regular letters. However, writing space is limited.

Addressing a Package

Address a package the same way you address a letter. Here are some things to keep in mind:

- **Write big.** Packages are usually larger than letter en-velopes, and you want to be sure the Postal Service can easily read the address. You might want to write with a marker instead of a ballpoint pen, so the writing will stand out.

- **Include messages for the letter carrier when needed.** If there is something breakable in the package, write FRAGILE on the outside. If the package contains pho-tographs or computer software, write PLEASE DO NOT BEND. Make sure you don't obscure the mailing ad-dress with your message.

- **Decide how you want to send the package.** Third class and book rate are cheaper than first class for send-ing a package, but it will take longer for the package to get there.

Part 5
Essays and Reports

Book Reports

Tips for Writing Good Book Reports

■ **Give yourself plenty of time.** Don't wait until the last minute to get started. Leave yourself time to think about the book (maybe even talk about it with some-one else) before you write your report.

■ **Choose a book that you think you'll like.** This may seem obvious, but it is surprising how little time some students spend selecting a book. And if the book you choose bores you, reading and reporting on it will definitely feel like a chore.

> Here are some tips:
>
> ■ Skim a few pages to see if you like the writing.
>
> ■ If you've read and enjoyed a book by an author, look for another book by the same person.
>
> ■ If you're looking for a nonfiction book, choose one on a topic you'd like to know more about.
>
> ■ Don't hesitate to ask your teacher or librarian for recommendations.

- **Read the entire book.** Don't just skim the whole book, or your book report will be superficial and weak.

- **Take notes as you read.** Jot down short notes on important things that happen in the story and to the characters. This will keep your thoughts organized and save you time later when you write your report. If there's a particular quote you want to repeat in your report, write down the page number so you can find it later. Remember, don't write or underline in a library book.

- **Summarize.** When writing your book report, don't try to tell everything that happens in the book. Give the highlights of the story. Concentrate on the main characters and what happens to them.

Reporting on a Work of Fiction

Four Parts of a Book Report

If your assignment is to write a short book report on a work of fiction, the teacher just wants to know that you've read the book and understood what it was about. It can be as short as a paragraph or as much as a page. Here are the parts of a short or long book report:

1. *Title*

The title of a book report is usually the title of the book (underlined or in all capital letters) followed by the author's name. If your teacher has a set format, follow it. And don't forget to include your name!

2. *Theme Statement*

The theme of the book should be stated in a sentence in the opening paragraph of your book report. The theme is usually the book's main idea.

Here are some questions you can ask yourself to figure out the main idea:

- **What did the central character in the story learn by the end?**

- **What was the author's main purpose in writing this book?**

- **What feeling or impression did you have when you finished reading the story?**

- **If someone asked you what this book was about, what would you say?**

---

3. Summary of the Story

The summary of the story tells about the plot. The plot is what happens to the main characters in the story. Your summary should have a beginning, middle, and end, just as the story does. Make sure you identify each character you name in the summary so your reader won't be confused.

4. Your Opinion

This statement of opinion is often called a critique. In a short book report, this should be stated briefly in a sentence or two.

Here is a short book report:

Your name	*Brian White*
The date	*March 15, 2000*
Title	*Justin and the Best Biscuits in the World*
	by
Author	*Mildred P. Walter*
Theme statement	*A good book to read is Justin and the Best Biscuits in the World by Mildred P. Walter. This book is about a ten-year-old boy whose grandfather is a cowboy.*
Summary	*This book was fun to read because Justin has two sisters who boss him around just like my sisters boss me. I know how he feels when everybody is on his case and always telling him what to do. Justin's sisters said he could not do anything right. But Justin's grandfather took him to his ranch and showed him how to clean*

his room, cook, and take care of himself. Now he can do something his sisters can't do. He can make the best biscuits in the world.

Brief personal opinion

I recommend this book to all the people in the world. This book will make you feel good.

Here is a two-page-long short book report:

Rebecca Halprin

November 5, 2000

<u>Banner in the Sky</u>
by
James Ramsey Ullman

<u>Banner in the Sky</u> is the story of a young boy who learns that being a man can mean giving up a dream for something more important.

Setting— place and time

Rudi Matt lives in a small village in the Swiss Alps in 1865. He dreams of climbing the Citadel, a high peak in the Alps. His father died trying to climb the Citadel fifteen years before. Rudi's mother and uncle won't let him try to climb the mountain. But John Winter, an English mountaineer, hires Rudi for his expedition up the Citadel. Rudi's uncle, Franz, also ends up going along as a guide.

Main characters identified

Winter is too exhausted to make it all the way to the top, and Franz stays behind to care for him. Another guide, Emil Saxo, goes ahead to the top with him.

When the two climbers meet on the mountain, Saxo tries to drive Rudi off and falls to a

Longer summary of story	*ledge, injured. Rudi must decide whether to help Saxo back to safety or to continue on to the summit. He brings Saxo down, allowing his uncle and John Winter to reach the summit. They plant Rudi's banner—his father's red flannel shirt—on the mountaintop in Rudi's honor.*
Personal opinion	*This was an exciting adventure story from beginning to end, and I enjoyed it very much. I would recommend it to anyone who likes a good adventure story.*

Long Book Reports

A long book report has the same four parts as a short one but retells the plot in depth, discusses the setting, and analyzes the characters. It also contains a fuller critique, your personal opinion, of the book.

Tips for Writing a Critique

Here are some questions to ask yourself as you write your critique:

- Did you enjoy the book? Why or why not?

- Did the story or characters remind you of your life? Did you identify with any of the characters?

- What did you notice about the author's style of writing?

- Was she or he particularly good at describing things or people? Writing dialogue? Creating suspense?

- If there are pictures in the book, how did they add to your enjoyment of the story?

- Would you recommend this book to a friend? Why or why not?

Here is a long book report on the same book:

Nathan Washington
September 30, 2000

Banner in the Sky
by
James Ramsey Ullman

    Banner in the Sky is the story of a young boy who learns that there are more ways than one to reach your dream.

    Rudi Matt lives in a tiny village in the Swiss Alps in 1865. What he wants most in the world is to climb the Citadel, a high peak in the Alps. Rudi's mother and his uncle, Franz, a mountain guide, want him to give up mountaineering and settle down to working in a hotel. Rudi will not give up his dream, however, and secretly signs on with John Winter, an English mountaineer, who is planning an expedition up the Citadel.

    Franz is furious when he finds out what Rudi has done, but he finally agrees to let his nephew go if he goes on the expedition, too. Franz also doesn't want to see Emil Saxo, a guide from another village whom Winter has hired, get to the top before him.

Longer summary of story

Rudi turns out to be a very good climber, but as they get close to the summit, Winter gets sick and can go no farther. Franz stays behind, loyal to Winter, but Saxo continues, determined to be the first on the summit. Rudi goes after Saxo, hoping to beat him to the top. When they meet, Saxo fights with Rudi and accidentally falls to a ledge below. Saxo is helpless and injured. Rudi must decide whether to carry Saxo back down to safety or to continue on alone to the summit.

He decides Saxo's life is more important than his dream and helps him down. In the meantime, Winter and Franz have continued the climb, and they reach the summit. Later, when they return to the village, Winter explains that Rudi is the real conqueror of the mountain because of his sacrifice. Through a telescope, Rudi is surprised to see his own banner—his father's red flannel shirt— flying on the mountaintop. Winter and Franz had planted it as a symbol of Rudi's triumph.

I enjoyed <u>Banner in the Sky</u> very much. Ullman, who was a mountain climber himself, writes about the thrill and danger of mountain climbing in a way that makes you feel you were on the expedition. The characters were interesting and acted like real people. Although I really identified with Rudi, I could understand how the other characters acted, even when Emil Saxo tried to hurt Rudi. The suspense of the final climb was totally exciting. I was sorry Rudi didn't get to the top of the mountain, but it was a good ending. I would recommend this book to anyone who likes a good adventure story about people who seem as real as you or me.

Critique and
supporting
details

165

Reporting on a Book You Didn't Like

Suppose you start a book for a report, thinking you'll like it. However, by the time you're finished, you find out you didn't like it at all. Now what do you do?

Here are some tips to keep in mind when writing a report about a book you didn't like:

- **Give your reasons.** It's not enough to simply say you didn't like the book. Give some good reasons for your opinion. Refer to the story, characters, and/or the author's style of writing.

- **Find something positive to say.** Few books are all bad. Try to find something you liked about the book—a character, an event, or some other aspect of the writing—to show you read it carefully enough to have a fair opinion.

- **Admit this is only your opinion.** Everyone has different tastes in literature. Try to think of the kind of person who might enjoy this story more than you did.

Here is a critique on the same book, but this writer didn't like it. The critique begins after the summary.

Reasons I
didn't like
book

One thing I
did like

Who might
like this book

I can't say that I enjoyed this book. It took way too long to get to the final mountain climb. Parts like when Rudi is visited by the spirit of his dead father in the cave were just too weird and didn't fit in with the rest of the book. And the ending was definitely disappointing.

Although I didn't like the book, I did enjoy some of the climbing scenes. They were realistic and exciting. I wish the rest of the book had been as exciting. However, if you're really into mountain climbing and don't mind books that take a while to get going, you might enjoy this book more than I did.

Reporting on a Work of Nonfiction

Nonfiction includes any story or essay that gives a description of a real event, place, or person.

Five Parts of a Nonfiction Book Report

1. Title

2. Theme Statement

> In a nonfiction book report, the title and theme statement are the same as in a report on a work of fiction.

3. Summary of the Book

The summary should cover the main sections of the book. Use the chapters as a guide to discussing the book's events in a logical order. This will also prevent you from getting bogged down in too many details.

4. Author's Purpose and Point of View

Although the book is factual, it is written from a particular point of view, the author's. In this part of your report, identify what the author's purpose is—to inform, persuade, teach, or entertain.

5. Your Opinion

In the final paragraph, write if you liked the book or not, and why. Also explain how well you think the author achieved his or her purpose.

Here are some questions you can ask yourself to help you write your critique:

- Did the author provide the information you were expecting to find in this book?

- Was the book written in an interesting and clear style?

- Do you have a better understanding of this subject after reading this book?

- If the author wanted to persuade you, were you convinced by his or her arguments?

- Would you recommend this book to anyone interested in this subject? Even to someone who knows nothing about it?

Here is a report on a biography:

Louis Penner
February 20, 2000

<u>And Then What Happened, Paul Revere?</u>
by
Jean Fritz

<u>And Then What Happened, Paul Revere?</u> is a biography of the American patriot and hero Paul Revere. Everybody knows about Paul Revere's midnight ride to warn the country that "The British are coming!" This entertaining book also talks about many other sides of Paul Revere.

At age fifteen, Revere took over his father's

Theme statement

Summary of events in person's life

silversmithing business. He later became a leader in opposing the British and was part of the Boston Tea Party in 1773. After his famous ride, Revere was a money printer, an engraver, a cannon maker, and a soldier. When the war ended and America won its independence, he returned to silversmithing and opened a hardware store. He lived to the ripe old age of 83.

Author's purpose

Mention illustrator

Jean Fritz's purpose in writing this book was to tell people more about an important American, and, at the same time, to tell an entertaining story. What I liked most about this book was the humor, both in the writing and the funny illustrations by Margot Tomes. Any kid who likes American history, especially the American Revolution, will enjoy this book. Kids who think history is boring might change their minds after reading this book.

Essays

An essay is a short composition that has one main idea. An essay may require research, and it often contains the writer's opinions, as well.

Three Kinds of Essays

Explanatory Essays

An explanatory essay tells about something or explains how to do something. Its purpose is to inform. It should be written in a straightforward, clear style. For example, you could write an essay called "Making Steam from Trash" in which you explain the technology used in burning garbage to make steam to create electricity.

Persuasive Essays

In a persuasive essay, the writer tries to persuade the reader to accept an idea or agree with an opinion. The writer's purpose is to convince the reader that her or his point of view is a reasonable one. The persuasive essay should be written in a style that grabs and holds the reader's attention, and the writer's opinion should be backed up by strong supporting details. You might write a persuasive essay on "Why Our School Library Should Remain Open After School."

Humorous Essays

A humorous essay takes a lighthearted look at its subject. This doesn't mean it is filled with jokes. It means that its main purpose is to entertain. In a humorous essay you might offer your zany idea on "How the Gladiator Became the Symbol of Laurel Middle School."

Steps to Follow When Writing Essays

- **Choose a topic carefully.** Pick a topic that interests you and that you know something about. Ideally, it is a subject or issue on which you have strong opinions.

- **Define your main idea.** Your main idea will help you focus your thoughts and research your topic. It is partly determined by your purpose—to inform, persuade, or entertain.

- **Organize the body of your essay carefully.** After gathering your research and ideas, make an outline. If your purpose is to persuade, place your most persuasive argument first and follow it with other arguments in order of importance. If your purpose is to inform, give each feature of your subject a paragraph to itself. If your purpose is to inform by instructing, order each step in sequence. Even a humorous essay should be organized so that the reader is swept into your point of view.

Four Parts of an Essay

All essays have four parts.

1. *Title*

The title should be descriptive and set the tone for the entire essay.

2. *Introduction*

The introduction is the first paragraph of an essay. Its purpose is to

- let the reader know the essay's purpose: to explain, persuade, or entertain.

- introduce the author's opinion and/or purpose.

- grab the reader's attention.

3. Body

The body explains or supports the main idea. It is usually several paragraphs long.

4. Conclusion

The conclusion repeats the main idea in a new way and brings the essay to a satisfying end.

Samples of Essays

Here is an explanatory essay:

Descriptive title

Important opening statistic

Important information

> ### Animal Testing
> By Jessica Parker
>
> Did you know that over five million animals are killed each year in laboratories for testing? Whenever you buy a product that has been tested on animals, you are supporting the killing of the kinds of animals that you might have for a pet.
>
> Rats, rabbits, mice, cats, dogs, birds, gerbils, and hamsters are being tested at this very moment. Over five hundred mice a day are being injected with window cleaner by a well-known manufacturer, for example. Rabbits are getting hot, melted lipstick forced into their eyes. If you wouldn't be willing to be treated like this, why should these animals be willing?

Steps to take

Here are some ways that you can prevent this cruelty:

1. Ask companies that test on animals to use a computerlike machine that is almost as accurate as an animal. They can use it over and over again.

2. Look at the labels of cosmetic products to see if they are tested on animals.

3. Ask the salesperson if the product is tested on animals.

4. Write letters to environmental groups, and ask about animal testing.

5. Join protests and rallies against animal testing.

6. Tell your friends what you have learned from these suggestions, or how they can help.

Conclusion

If enough people protest this cruelty to animals, maybe we can stop it.

Here is an explanatory essay by a younger writer:

Spoolmobile
by
Erica Sterling

When our class made spoolmobiles, we had a lot of fun doing it. It was really easy. First you take a rubber band and put it around a straw. Then you take a washer and put it through the rubber band. Next take the rubber band and stick it through the spool. Then you take a stirrer and cut it and stick it through the rubber band. Last, take a piece of tape and put it on the stirrer. When you finish it, put it on the ground and turn the straw and let go of it, and it should roll. The more you spin it, the more it will roll. I really enjoyed doing it. It is a fun project.

Here is a persuasive essay:

Nonviolence: Making It Work Today
Example: Environmental Violence
by
Tim Ruggeri

Main idea
sentence

 There are many problems in the world today that can't be helped, but some problems can be solved. Environmental violence is one that can. People dumping waste and killing animals can be stopped, but only with a lot of people's help. I am writing this essay so I can tell you about some of these issues, like killing animals, or offshore dumping, and how they can be

Naming an
authority

stopped. It think this goes with Martin Luther King's second principle: The beloved community is a world of peace with justice.

Argument

 People killing endangered animals are doing something that is hurting others. Pretty soon they might find themselves killing the last of *that species. All kinds of animals, even our nation's bird, the bald eagle, are becoming extinct and they must be helped.*

Another important environmental violence issue is that some people don't know what to do with toxic waste so they just dump it in the ocean, not thinking about what they have just done. They have just contaminated our ocean and probably killed a lot of animals that live in the water. People also dump garbage in the water that some animals will think is food, and when they eat it they will die because they will choke.

Conclusion

Martin Luther King believed that communities should work together to make peace, and people dumping waste and killing animals aren't doing what he is saying. This affects me because the pollution will be there for years to come unless someone stops this. There are not many ways to stop this, but there are a couple of possible solutions. One of them is to write letters to Congress to try to pass a new law to fine anybody who is caught doing any of these bad deeds. Another is to donate some money to a wildlife refuge.

Here are two humorous essays:

Creative title

Tales From the Chair
by R. Katie Barnes

Clever
introduction

Junior High means more than just lockers and desks; for us unfortunate many with un perfect teeth, it also means braces. I've had my braces since I was four and am getting ready to celebrate a decade of dental wear! Yay! It's not just the gumlessness, aching, or wire, not even the ability to pick up radio signals in my mouth that makes braces so annoying. It's the dreaded CHECKUP!

Main idea

It's pretty routine. My mom takes me out of my favorite class (lunch) so that I can go to the dentist's office. Once I'm there, I sit for an hour in an uncomfortable chair, staring at the latest issue of Bug Collector's Monthly *, until a perky woman in a blue suit and plastered smile calls me into the dentist's room. Before I know it, another woman has come in and whisked a bib around my neck, and has a 1,000,000-watt bulb shining in my eyes. Then she inserts a device into my mouth that greatly stretches apart my lips and surrounding facial structures, until they are pressed firmly against my ears. She then asks me my name, what grade I'm in, what school I go to, how old I am, and anything else*

Increasing
exaggeration

she can think of, as if I can answer with half of my face immobilized. Then, she whips out a miniature monkey wrench and directs it towards my now overstretched mouth. After several futile attempts, she manages to pull out the wrong thing.

"Oops," she giggles. "Better get that blood."

Before I have time to make a break for it, the head dentist enters. I am content to let him examine my battered mouth, because a visit by the head dentist usually means the end is near. He then leaves me in the incompetent hands of the dreaded cheerful assistant. She tries to make pleasant conversation as she destroys what few teeth I have left. She babbles on and on, and I try to tune her out. She apparently thinks of me as teeth with ears.

Several hours and about 300 mistakes later, she's done. I am whisked to the waiting room where my mom seems grateful to see me. Perhaps she heard my muffled screams of anguish. I look at her watch to see how many days I've been there. 12:30! That can't be! I haven't even missed algebra!

As I approach the door that leads to sunshine and freedom, the office assistant hands me a balloon. "Please come again," she pipes in her sickeningly sweet voice. The balloon has a large smiley face on it, and I decide to keep it in my room, as a reminder of what lies in the future—my fateful trip back to THE CHAIR. . . .

Ridiculous
conclusion

Jennifer Brehm   March 12, 2000
Writing   Ms. Mastrandrea

The Human Clock

Hi! I am a time. I know because everyone always points to me and says, "Look at the time!" They say time flies when you're having fun, but I most certainly do not fly. I sit pinned to the wall. I hate it when people turn my wheel because my hands turn all over my face and it twists my nose around. So I get back at them! I make good times go fast and bad times go slow. On a special night, all times go back an hour. This makes people get mixed up with the time.

I work in a very unique way, as I have three hands. My second hand is always in a hurry to get somewhere, and my hour hand thinks he has all the time in the world. I like my minute hand. She's just right.

Once I saw a poor little time strapped to a person. He looked sad because he was strapped onto this person so he couldn't move. I then told him about my grandfather who is so bossy and has such a loud voice. Next I told him about the times who are chained to people, so he would know he wasn't the only one that was sad. There are others with the same feelings just like he has. Finally, I told him how I felt when the kids at school scream and run away at the end of the day, leaving me alone. This makes me feel like I am a monster. This is my life as a clock. Sometimes it's interesting, sometimes it's not.

Answering Essay Test Questions

Essay test questions are in-depth questions that cannot be answered in a few words, but require at least a paragraph. Like an essay, an essay question has a main idea that you must recognize to answer the question fully and satisfactorily.

Here are some useful tips for writing answers to essay test questions:

- **Read directions and questions carefully.** To answer a question concisely, look for clue words that indicate how a question should be answered. These words include explain, compare, illustrate, summarize, and contrast.

- **Restate the question as a declarative sentence.** If the question says, "Why did the American colonists oppose the Stamp Act? Give at least two reasons," your answer might begin, "The two most important reasons that American colonists opposed the Stamp Act were . . ."

- **Be concise and focused.** Avoid including unnecessary information. Don't repeat yourself. Answer the question as thoroughly as you can and then move on to the next one.

- **Use scratch paper, if allowed, for writing down ideas.** This will enable you to jot down thoughts or outline your answers without messing up your test page.

> ■ **Leave time to go over your finished work.**
> **Allow yourself time to go back and make—**
> **as neatly as possible—any necessary correc-**
> **tions in punctuation, grammar, or spelling.**

Here are three essay test questions and their answers:

Clue word

<u>Describe</u> how you might feel if you were rescued from slavery by Harriet Tubman. What are you thinking? What are you doing? Where are you?

Descriptive scene

I was just getting to sleep when someone knocked on the door. My mom went to get it. "It's Moses!" she cried. "You've come to get us!"

"Shh!" the person at the door said. "Now get your things. We're going on a long trip."

Who, what and where

I packed up some of my stuff, and we set out to the North. At first I thought we had been sold, but when I saw the lady's face I knew we were fine. It was Harriet Tubman. As we were walking, I heard hooves. We were being chased. I hurried up a little. At about 5:00 A.M. we laid down on the moss and went to sleep. We could only travel at night.

Supporting details

When I woke up it was midnight. We still had a few hundred miles to go. We had a breakfast of nuts and berries. We finally got to a station where the people gave us food and directions. We were still miles away from Canada.

On Friday we made it. We crossed the Mason-Dixon line, and we were free. I was so happy, I hugged Harriet. It felt so good to be free!

Clue word

Using wording
of the
question

Good
examples

Interesting
fact

Defining
term to
show
understanding

<u>Describe</u> the main characteristics of mammals.

There are four main characteristics of mammals that make them different from all other animals. Mammals nurse their young and take care of them longer than other animals. Mother's milk is the first food for human babies, as well as dogs and cats. Opossums and kangaroos are so protective of their young that they carry them around in a pouch. Mammals are the only animals that have hair on their bodies. Some are covered with thick hair, like bears, while others only have hair at certain times of life. Some whales only have hair before they are born. Mammals have bigger and more highly developed brains than other creatures. Among the most intelligent are humans, pigs, dolphins, and apes. Finally, all mammals are warm-blooded. This means their body temperature stays about the same even if the temperature around them changes.

Clue word

Explain what it would be like to live in King Arthur's time.

Use wording of question

In King Arthur's time you couldn't just go to the fridge or the bathroom for water. You had to go to a stream or a well. And you couldn't watch cable TV! Boy, what torture! The only book to read was the Bible. They didn't have printers back then, either. A nun or a monk might spend forty years copying the Bible.

Interesting fact

Back then, some people were accused of being witches. If you were accused, the people would give you the water test. They would throw you in the water. If you drowned, you were innocent. If you stayed afloat, you were burned at the stake. Only a witch could float!

Writing Science Reports

A science research report can be one of three kinds:

- an account of an experiment
- an exploration of a topic of scientific interest
- the story of a scientist's life and work

Reporting on an Experiment

A report on an experiment has three basic parts: the hypothesis, the experiment, and the conclusion.

1. Hypothesis

A hypothesis is a statement that can be tested by an experiment to see if it is true. You should state your hypothesis simply and directly in a sentence. It should be preceded by the word Hypothesis and a colon. For example:

> *Hypothesis: Mold grows more easily under warm, moist conditions than under cool, dry conditions.*

2. Experiment

The experiment part consists of three sections:

- the list of materials you used
- the numbered steps you performed
- the results

3. Conclusion

In the conclusion, you tell what the experiment shows and how it proves or disproves your original hypothesis.

Each action you perform is a separate step. Write each step clearly and simply. Take notes during the experiment so you don't forget anything.

Here is a report on an experiment on salt and ice:

An Experiment on Salt and Ice
by
Roger Nelson

Hypothesis

HYPOTHESIS: Salt lowers the melting point of water and can be used effectively to melt ice.

EXPERIMENT

List of materials

MATERIALS: a glass of water, a piece of string several inches long, an ice cube, a filled saltshaker

PROCEDURE:

Steps listed clearly

1. *I placed the ice cube on the surface of the water-filled glass.*
2. *Next I tied a 1-inch loop in the piece of string and held the string over the ice cube so the loop end touched the top of it.*
3. *Then I shook some salt on top of the ice cube where the loop of string sat. I waited for a few minutes.*

Results

4. *I picked up the string. The loop stuck to the cube, and I could lift it right out of the water glass.*

Relates results to hypothesis

CONCLUSION: The salt caused the ice to melt around the string. Then the water froze again and froze the string to the ice cube. This is why I was able to lift up the string with the ice cube attached. The results of the experiment prove my hypothesis that salt is an effective ice melter.

Reporting on a Research Topic

This kind of report can be on any science topic, such as:

- weather conditions

- geological features

- animals

- plants and trees

- space exploration

- electricity

- the environment

- computer technology

Here are some tips for writing a research report on a science topic:

- **Narrow your topic.** This can't be emphasized enough. Many students take on a topic that is too general or too large to cover comfortably in one report. Animals is obviously too broad a topic, but so might be animals of Australia. A more focused topic would be one particular Australian animal, such as the koala bear, the kangaroo, or the platypus.

- **Use periodicals in your research.** Scientific knowledge is always expanding. Consult newspapers, recent scientific magazines, such as *Popular Science* and *Natural History*, and those written for young readers, such as *Science News* and *Science World*.

> ■ **Include a visual aid in your report.** A
> chart, diagram, or photograph can give your
> reader a better understanding of the topic.
> For example, if you were doing a report on a
> plant or animal, you might include a dia-
> gram naming all its parts.

Three Parts of a Report on a Topic

1. Introduction

The introduction presents your main idea about the
topic and sets the tone for the entire report. It should
capture your reader's interest immediately.

**Here is an introduction to a report on a research topic,
the platypus:**

The Incredible Platypus
by
Martin Slotkin

Dramatic opening

    *Near the end of the 18th century, the skin of a
strange animal arrived from Australia at a labo-
ratory in London, England. The animal had the
bill and webbed feet of a duck and the skin of a
beaver. Some scientists who saw the skin called
it a hoax. But one man, Dr. Irving Shaw, believed it was real. He named the animal platy-*

Suspense

*pus, which is Greek for "flat-footed." Nearly two
hundred years later, the platypus is still one of*

Main idea

the strangest animals on earth.

2. Body

The body of the report contains information and details that tell about the topic and support the main idea.

- It should have a topic sentence that the other sentences relate to or support.

- Each paragraph should follow the next in a logical, organized sequence.

- The body of a research topic report discusses different aspects of the topic.

- The body of a report on a person follows the person's life, focusing on his or her scientific achievements. Enrich the body with quotes and visual aids.

Here is the body of the report on the platypus:

Topic sentence	*The platypus may look like a helpless animal, but it isn't. All male platypuses have a hollowed, clawlike projection called a "spur" on*
Term defined	*their hind legs. It is connected to glands that secrete poison. Scientists believe the platypus uses the spur for defense. The poison is not deadly, but drugs a victim when it is ejected*
Supporting details	*through the spur into the prey's skin. One man hit in the hand by a platypus's spur couldn't move his hand for nine weeks!*

3. Conclusion

The conclusion brings the report to a satisfactory end by summarizing the main idea in a few well-chosen sentences.

Here is the conclusion of the report on the platypus:

Repetition of main idea

Satisfying closing

> *The platypus is truly an amazing creature. With all its oddities, this animal is well adapted to its environment. Although it is believed by scientists to be among the most primitive of mammals, the platypus is an animal whose mysteries are only beginning to be understood.*

Here is a short science report on a sea horse by a young writer:

Title states the topic

Main idea

Supporting facts

> *About the Sea Horse*
> *by*
> *Amanda Altman*
>
> A sea horse is a very weird kind of fish. It moves only a few times a minute. It swims by grabbing on to plants and moving the fin on its back. One amazing thing is that the sea horse moves its back fin 60 times per second. They have two skeletons, which most fish don't have. Sea horses eat little green shrimp. The biggest a sea horse can grow is two feet.

Reporting on a Person

A report on a scientist should give the reader an understanding of events in the person's life that influenced her or his career in science. It should explain some of the work the scientist has done. The parts of this report are the same as for a report on a topic: introduction, body, conclusion. Look for information on writing a report on a person in the next section on social studies reports.

Writing Social Studies Reports

Three kinds of social studies reports are:

- on a place
- on a social issue
- on a person

Reporting on a Place

You might want to write a report on a place you would like to visit someday, such as the pyramids of Egypt or the outback of Australia. Or, you might want to report on someplace close to home, such as the state capital or a Revolutionary War battlefield.

> **Either way, here are some questions to answer as you plan your report on a place:**
>
> - **Where is this place?**
> - **What are the geographic features and climate of this place? How do these affect the people and wildlife that live in or near it?**
> - **What other places border on this place? How does location influence the place and its neighbors?**
> - **What kind of people, if any, live in this place? How do they live? What do they do for a living? What are their homes like?**

> - **What is the historical background of this place? How does its past affect its present?**
>
> - **Have you visited this place? If so, what are your personal impressions?**

Possible subtopics for a report on a country or state

If the place you choose for a topic is a country or state, here are some subtopics you may want to include in your report:

- location

- cities

- people

- natural resources

- form of government

- settlement and history

- industry and agriculture

- religion

- food

- climate

If you discover there is too much material for one report, narrow your topic to one aspect of a country or a state, such as the natural resources of Spain or the Native American culture of New Mexico.

Reporting on a Social Issue

Newspapers, magazines, and television news will provide you with many ideas for this kind of report.

Here are a few:

- gun control
- health care
- population control
- education
- the environment
- censorship
- children's rights
- consumer protection
- influence of media
- the homeless

Here are some useful tips to keep in mind when writing a report on a social issue:

- **Show all sides.** If the issue you are reporting about is a controversial one, present all sides of the issue. This way readers can make up their own minds. You may present your own point of view in the conclusion.

- **Use up-to-date sources of information.** Don't confine your research to books and encyclopedias. Use magazines, newspapers, radio, and television to make sure your research is up-to-date and relevant.

- **Include statistics and visual aids in your report.** Visual aids that clearly illustrate your points can make your report more effective. Good visual aids for a social studies report include maps, charts, and time lines.

Reporting on a Person

A social studies report can be about a person who is famous, or an ordinary person whose experiences were important in history or the news.

Here are some of the different kinds of people you might consider:

- soldiers

- business leaders

- explorers

- political figures

- athletes

- journalists

- writers and artists

- community leaders

- thinkers and educators

- religious leaders

- entertainers

- activists in social movements

> **Here are some tips to keep in mind when writing a report on a person:**
>
> - **Choose someone you admire.** If you like the person you've chosen, you're more likely to write a report that is interesting and informative.

- **Use primary sources whenever possible.** A primary source is something spoken or written by the person or someone who knew her or him personally. Good primary sources include autobiographies, letters, quotes in contemporary newspaper and magazine articles, and personal interviews. When quoting from a primary source, make sure you give the source credit in your text and in your bibliography (include the author, work, and page number). Also be sure to put quotation marks around the person's exact words.

- **Highlight any events in the person's life that helped ensure his or her success.**

- **Discuss setbacks that may have taught the person an important lesson.**

- **Stress the person's achievements.** Focus on what this person did that is worth the reader's attention.

Three Parts of Any Social Studies Report

1. Introduction

The introduction to a social studies report presents the topic, whether it be a place, issue, or person. Present your topic in a way that makes your reader want to know more about it. This may be done with a dramatic scene, a descriptive picture, or a startling statistic. Your introduction should also contain the main idea about the topic that you will further explain and explore in the rest of the report.

Here is an introduction for a report on a place:

Inside the Sahara
by
Amy Dubcek

Descriptive word picture

Amazing statistic

Suspense-building lead-in

> *It is three and a half million square miles of sand, rocks, plateaus, and mountains about the size of the United States. It covers parts of ten countries, but its main inhabitants are snakes, lizards, and gerbils. Much of it gets less than one inch of rain a year. The highest temperature on record, 136°F, was recorded there. Its name means "desert" in Arabic. It is the Sahara, the world's largest desert.*

Here is an introduction for a report on an issue:

Elisabeth Kiernan
Grade 4
Babylon Grade School

Pulling Together in the Face of Disaster

Strong dramatic opener

On August 24, 1992, Hurricane Andrew struck Homestead, Florida. Homestead was destroyed. The land and homes were ruined. The wind speeds from this storm were up to one hundred and four miles per hour.

Startling statistics

After the storm, the results were devastating. Eighty-five thousand homes were destroyed. One hundred eighty thousand residents were left homeless. Hurricane Andrew left twenty billion dollars in damages and repairs.

Here is an introduction for a report on a person:

Benjamin Banneker
by
Kelly Thompson

Dramatic opener

President George Washington was worried. The fate of the future capital of the United States was in jeopardy. The architect of the new city of Washington, Major Pierre Charles L'Enfant, had just quit the project and taken all his plans with him. It would take years to build a city without those plans.

As the President expressed his fears to the team that had been working with L'Enfant, an assistant surveyor quietly said he knew all of L'Enfant's plans by memory and could reproduce them. The President was amazed, but the surveyor soon proved what he said was true.

Effective summary of achievements

African-American Benjamin Banneker— astronomer, almanac summary writer, mathematician, and surveyor—was about to add another triumph to his list of achievements: U.S. capital builder.

2. *Body*

The body of the report expands and explores the topic.

■ In a report about a place, the body describes features of the place. These may be in separate paragraphs or even separated by subtopic headings.

■ In a report about an issue, the issue may be examined from both pro and con positions.

■ In a report on a person, the person's life and achievements are explored in chronological order.

Here is a paragraph from the body of the report on the Sahara (cont'd from page 196):

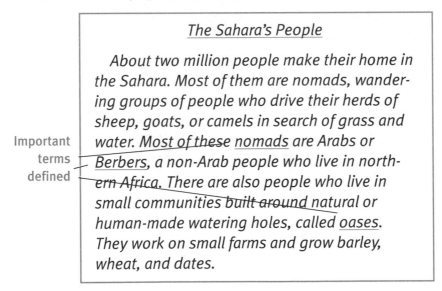

The Sahara's People

About two million people make their home in the Sahara. Most of them are nomads, wandering groups of people who drive their herds of sheep, goats, or camels in search of grass and water. Most of these <u>nomads</u> are Arabs or <u>Berbers</u>, a non-Arab people who live in northern Africa. There are also people who live in small communities built around natural or human-made watering holes, called <u>oases</u>. They work on small farms and grow barley, wheat, and dates.

Important terms defined

Here is a part of the body of the report on Hurricane Andrew (cont'd from page 196):

Topic sentence of paragraph

Some people coped well, and others didn't. Some people started looting because there wasn't electricity, and at night when everything was dark, people could not watch over their homes or stores unless they stayed up all night. Looters carried guns and took whatever they could. Fighting and violence took place.

The Red Cross and the National Guard soon came through. They brought shelters, clothing, food, and water to Florida. So many people were homeless and starving that tent cities were set up. Tent cities gave the people homes. Food was given out buffet-style.

Here is a paragraph from the body of the report on Benjamin Banneker (cont'd from page 197):

Important episode from youth

When Benjamin Banneker was young, you could already tell that he would be someone special. Once, an old man gave Benjamin a pocket watch as a present. Benjamin took it apart to see how it worked and put it back together. A local schoolteacher who lived near Benjamin's farm in Maryland gave him a journal with a diagram of a clock. Benjamin used the diagram and his pocket watch as models for building his own clock. He made the whole thing out of wood. It took him two years to finish. It

> *was the first clock built in the U.S., and people came from all over the Middle Colonies to see it. It kept nearly perfect time for over fifty years.*

3. Conclusion

In a social studies report on a place or a person, the conclusion repeats the main idea and sums up what you have to say about your topic. In a report on an issue, the conclusion can sum up the different sides, present your personal feelings and thoughts, and offer possible solutions.

Here is a conclusion for the report on the Sahara Desert (cont'd from page 198):

Possible future developments

Restatement of main idea

> *Over centuries the Sahara has gotten drier and larger. Some experts feel the Sahara is still expanding because there are droughts on the southern border. Other people claim the droughts are part of the natural cycle of the desert. Either way, the Sahara is one of the world's toughest and most amazing environments.*

Here is a conclusion for the report on Hurricane Andrew (cont'd from page 199):

> *Even today the people in Florida still haven't recovered, but everyone can learn from this disaster. Instead of violence, people should always try to work things out peacefully. I really learned from this lesson. I hope you have, too.*

Here is a conclusion for the report on Benjamin Banneker (cont'd from pages 199–200):

Final
summary of
achievements

Topic
sentence of
report
reworded

> *Benjamin Banneker died in 1806, but his legacy lives on today. He was the most famous African American of his day and for good reason. He built the first clock in the United States. He helped build our permanent capital city. He predicted an eclipse of the sun. He wrote one of the most popular almanacs in the United States. He spoke out against slavery in letters to the United States' third president, Thomas Jefferson. Benjamin Banneker was truly a great American.*

Here is a complete report on a person with an unusual approach. The writer chose to write as if Annie Sullivan were telling her own story.

> *Annie Sullivan*
> *by Alex Brucculari*
>
> *I'm Annie Sullivan. When I was a child my eyes weren't too good, and when I started to rub them they got red. I lived in a poor family. I was born April 14, 1866. I was baptized by the name of Joanna, but everyone called me Annie.*
> *I was brought to a poorhouse when I was ten because my parents had died. I had a brother named Jimmie. He was younger than I and had a lump on his hip. That's how our mother died. I was very small for my age and didn't know how old I was, so the people at the poorhouse*

guessed my age. They thought I was eight, but I was really ten.

One time in the middle of the night, I woke up and found my brother dead. I screamed and cried and woke the whole poorhouse. Lights came on, and people ran to help me. I didn't know they were there to help me. I thought they were going to take me away. I started to bite and cried harder. For the next couple of days I had to cry myself to sleep.

When I was old enough to get a job I was blind. I got some operations. The second operation worked. My vision was blurry, but at least I could see. Later I got glasses and could see very well.

I went to school, and when I graduated I got another job. It was teaching a deaf, blind, and mute little girl, Helen Keller. Helen's mother and father felt bad for her and let her eat off other people's plates. I had to teach her not to and even had to grab her. It took a long time before I could actually teach Helen things.

Finally, we were out pumping water when I thought about it. I took Helen's hand and put it under the water so she could feel it and know what it was by feeling. It took lots of patience. Finally, we started to talk with our hands. I graduated with Helen and managed to help her finish her last book. Then on October 19, 1936, I died.

Here is a complete report on the Shoshoni:

How the Shoshoni Got Their Food
by Ben Pred

Shoshoni lived in the mountains where there was not much food. In the mountains they ate squirrels, grasshoppers, sheep, antelope, and birds. Once a year or so, the Shoshoni would go to the plains for a buffalo hunt. Some would go to the woods for seeds, berries, and small birds. Another group would go swimming for salmon.

Some Shoshoni used branches or animal hides to build their homes. Some Shoshoni dug shelters in the hillside. They played a kind of football with a ball made of animal skin stuffed with rabbit hair. But they didn't have much time to play. They had to build their homes and find food. In many ways, the Shoshoni had it much harder than the Iroquois. The Iroquois had salmon, deer, and other fish and animals. The Shoshoni only went hunting once a year, and they ate grasshoppers. I think I would have liked to be an Iroquois.

Bibliographies

When you do research for a paper, you can look in books, magazines, newspapers, or on the Internet. You may search for information on a CD-ROM, or you may even interview someone. At the end of your paper, you must tell where you got all your facts. A bibliography is a list of all the sources you used to write your paper. The bibliography contains important facts, such as the names of authors, the titles of books, and publishing information (where the book was published, who published it, and when).

Each item in a bibliography must be punctuated in a certain way. Here are the ways to punctuate the most common sources for a research paper.

When you list several sources in a bibliography, list them in alphabetical order by the author's last name or by the first word in the entry. Indent all lines after the first.

Note: None of the bibliographical entries given as examples below is real. They are all made up. The titles that are in italics in the entries below could also be underlined without italics.

Books

You must always give three pieces of information about a book you used: author or authors (followed by a period), title of book (in italics or underlined, followed by a period), and publishing information (followed by a period).

Here is how to list a book written by one author:

Author's last name, author's first name. *Title of book.* City of publication: name of publisher, date of publication.

Banter, Nej. *Fantastic Jewelry Designs.* New York: Silversmith Publishing, Inc., 1976.

If there are two or three authors, list the first author's last name and the name(s) of the other author(s) in regular order.

Two authors:

Jordan, Sandra, and Mike L. Angelo. *What's Under the Paint.* Rome: Easel Books, 1929.

Three authors:

Taraban, Samuel, Sara Gillets, and Albert Katz. *Our Wonderful Son.* Chelsea, MA: Shawmut Books, 1940.

If a book has more than three authors, write just the first author's name (last name, comma, first name) and the Latin words **et al.** (which means "and others") for the other authors. The rest of the entry is the same as for books by one, two, or three authors.

Norfox, Harry, et al. *Punctuation Drives Me Crazy.* Chicago: Punc Publishers, 1998.

Magazine Articles

Author's last name, author's first name. "Title of article." *Name of magazine.* Volume number (if any). Date of publication: page number(s).

Seuling, Barbara. "Wacky Laws I Have Often Broken." *United States Official Law Journal.* July 22, 2000: 320–322.

Newspaper Articles

Author's last name, author's first name. "Title of article." *Name of newspaper.* Date of publication, section and page number.

Manushkin, Fran. "Great Animals of the Bible." *The Chicago Gazette.* Nov. 2, 1999, G 44.

Personal Interviews

Last name of person interviewed, first name of person interviewed. "Personal interview." Date of interview.

Lerangis, Peter. Personal interview. Aug. 19, 1998.

The Internet

When you do research on the Internet, give as much information in your bibliography about your source as you can. Put angle brackets (< >) around the Internet address. (It's a good idea to print out the material you are using. It may not still be available on the Internet if you have to find it again.)

Author's last name (if given), author's first name (if given). "Title of article." Internet: <Internet address> Date you got the information.

Bryant, Bonnie. "Horses With Their Saddles Off." Internet: <http://www.whinnyandneigh.com> May 21, 2000.

Computer Software (CD-ROMs, Disks, etc.)

Author's last name (if given), author's first name (if given). *Title of Software.* Computer software. Name of publisher, copyright date or date of publication. Type of software (CD-ROM, disk, etc.).

Levine, Ellen. *Adventures on 101st Street.* Computer software. Koedt Edutainment, 2001. CD-ROM.

Part 6
Writing Skills

Planning Your Work

Getting Started

It's difficult to write well when you're staring at the clock instead of the page. Writing takes a lot of time. Plan ahead so that you have enough time to produce the best writing you can create.

If you play a sport, you know that you play best when your body is warmed up. Writing is a mental exercise in the same way that dance and football are physical exercises. Your mind needs to warm up in order for you to write well. The first few minutes of writing may be the most difficult. This is why it is important that you do not interrupt yourself while in the act of writing. If you do, you will have to warm up all over again.

> *Writing well is a skill, much like other skills, in which preparation cannot be overlooked or faked.*

Imagine for a moment that you are on the basketball court right in the middle of a layup, when you have to stop everything and look for something. When you've found it, can you go right back into the middle of the layup? Of course not. You have to wait for your chance to do another layup all over again. When you're in the middle of writing a report and you stop because a friend calls or you need to find an eraser, you are interrupting yourself from writing the best you can.

This chapter will focus on how to prepare to write by organizing yourself and your ideas before you start. You will be able to see that some of the writer's most important work is done before putting pen to paper.

Find a Place and Time

Your workplace needs to be in an area that allows you to think. Separate yourself from the noise of radios and televisions and the voices of other people. A table or desk with good light puts you in the ideal position for thinking and writing. Clear the surface of clutter before sitting down to write. You wouldn't play basketball on a court strewn with half-full cans of soda, and you wouldn't pirouette across a floor cluttered with papers and pens. A clean and neat desk will help you to concentrate; a cluttered and messy desk will distract you.

Are you at your best right after you get home from school, or are you more alert early in the morning? Most people find that they concentrate best at a specific time of day. Give yourself every advantage of planning to write during that time.

Have Your Tools Ready

If you're lucky enough to have your own writing desk or table, you will be able to organize it so that everything you need is at your fingertips.

If your workplace, however, is the kitchen table, you can keep most of your writing tools in a handy box or basket that can be set up at a moment's notice.

It's important to have your tools ready before you start to write because, if you don't, you will have to stop writing to go on a treasure hunt for your eraser or dictionary. This will waste time and will waste something even more precious: your train of thought.

Wherever you write, be sure that you have the following items close at hand:

- pens and pencils

- erasers

- writing paper and scratch paper

- reference books, such as a dictionary, thesaurus, ency-
clopedia, and a style guide

- a computer or a typewriter, if you use one

What Are You Writing?

Now that you are stationed at your uncluttered desk with
your mind clear and fresh and all your tools ready, it is
time to get down to business.

Write your assignment at the top of the page or the computer screen. Make sure that you write it down accurately.
Read the assignment over to yourself several times and decide exactly what it is that you are being asked to do.

Writing assignments take different forms. Below are the
most common types of writing assignments and what they
expect of the writer.

- **Reports** pass along information to others.
   The report may be about something you have read or
   something you have seen or done. For example, you
   might report on *Little Women* by Louisa May Alcott or
   on your trip to City Hall.

- **Reviews** give your opinion about or reaction to an
   event or performance.
   You might write a review of the movie *Indian in the
   Cupboard* or of a performance by the school orchestra.
   If you write a review (rather than a report) about a book
   you have read, most of the writing will concern your
   personal reaction.

- **Essays** are carefully shaped pieces of writing around a central theme or idea.

  These may be factual statements or personal opinion. You might write an essay about the beginning of school or about the importance of recycling. Essays often attempt to persuade the reader of the writer's opinion, but they may simply paint a picture in words about an experience or feeling.

- **Stories** tell about real or imaginary happenings.

  In nonfiction, you may describe a personal experience in the form of a story using details, remembered conversation, and your memory.

  In fiction, you can explore the personalities of the characters and communicate the feel of the place, or setting, where the story is happening. The plot can be outlandish, exciting, and utterly untrue. For example, you might write a story called *My Trip to Mars*.

- **Plays** are stories told through dialogue and action.

  What characters say and do moves the action along.

- **Poems** are stories or thoughts written in strong rhythm with special attention to the sound of the words.

  Think of poems as the most concentrated of writing forms. Poems are often written in rhyme, but other poems, sometimes called free verse or blank verse, have no rhymes.

Do Your Research

Many writing assignments require research. Think about what you need to do for a particular assignment and organize your workload accordingly.

- For a book report, read the book and make notes of the main points and your reactions to them.

- For a **research report**, look up your topic in all the reference sources you can find. Visit the local library and ask a librarian for assistance in finding the materials you need.

- For a **report on a science experiment**, use the notes you made while the experiment was in progress.

- For **creative writing**, such as short stories and poems, use your journal or other personal experiences for ideas that are yours alone. Talk to others about their experiences, which you can then interpret in your own words. When writing about relatives, you can arrange to interview them. Take notes during the interview and use them in your writing.

- For an **essay**, understand the assignment (to inform, to convince, to entertain). Depending on the purpose, do research, rely on your own experience, and decide how you feel about the topic.

Brainstorm for Ideas

Now that you understand the assignment and have done your research, you can brainstorm for ideas about what you are going to write.

Brainstorming is a lot of fun. Write down whatever enters your head on the subject. Do not worry about spelling or grammar or incomplete sentences while brainstorming. No one will read this except you. The point is to get all your ideas onto paper, so that you can begin to work with them.

For instance, this list contains the highlights of a trip one student took to India.

- Left O'Hare International Airport early one June morning

- Traveled with my family

- Like 24 hours in a coma

- Landed at Indira Gandhi International in New Delhi at 3 A.M.

- Chaos of Indian cities contrasts with serene country-side

- Stop at Haradwar, holy city on the Ganges

- Why Hindus bathe in the Ganges

- I walk down marble steps through crowds of beggars and take the plunge

Before You Begin, Make a Plan

Coaches always give a game plan to their players before sending them onto the field. Writers also need to organize what they're going to do before they try to do it. When you have brainstormed for ideas, look over your notes and organize your thoughts. Whether you use a formal outline or some other organizer, a plan is an essential step toward writing with style. You need one whether you're writing a book report, a poem, a letter to a grandparent, or your autobiography. Without an outline, you are likely to leave things out or jump from one idea to another too quickly. It may seem as though making a plan adds an extra step, but it will actually save you time. It is a lot easier to write what you have to say when you know what you have to say!

In an outline or graphic organizer, you decide what you are going to say without having to write down every word. Each paragraph then logically follows the next, and the writing itself becomes easier.

There are three popular ways of planning.

■ **Word clusters** are good for poems and essays.
These word clusters form the organization of a poem Cassidy wrote:

Poems are like going through doors to rooms.

Room 1	Room 2	Room 3
golden sunlight	*violets in every window*	*goldenrod*
	always June	*a silver snake*
shadows	*colored birds*	*water lilies*
	spiderwebs	*tiny people writing poetry*

■ **Venn diagrams** help you organize plots and facts and may help you see new relationships between various characters.

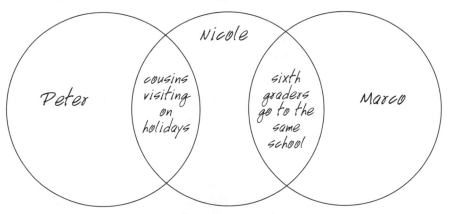

■ **Straightforward outlines** help give form to reports and nonfiction stories. They may also help you build a structure for a play.
Here is an outline Ben wrote about the author Madeleine L'Engle:

I. *Who is Madeleine L'Engle?*
   A. *What did she write?*
   B. *How did she become famous?*
      1. *A Wrinkle in Time*
      2. *An interesting point about the fate of her most famous book*

II. *Her childhood:*
   A. *She was considered stupid by her teachers and mocked by them.*
   B. *She was fiercely intelligent.*
   C. *No one, not even her mother, knew just how clever she was.*

III. *Madeleine today:*
   A. *Where does she live?*
   B. *What is she doing?*

What you plan to write will help you decide which kind of plan works best. The important thing is to organize your ideas to ensure that you won't leave out any important information.

With your workplace organized, mind and spirit raring to go, and your plan perfected, you are ready for the fun part. Ready, set, write!

Producing Your Work

Beginning to Write

You have found the ideal place and time to work, completed your research, and made a plan. You can now begin to write. You know what you want to say and in what order you want to say it. But how will you put your ideas into words that will be exciting to read?

Writing well is a lot like learning how to play an instrument well. It requires practice. It doesn't matter how easily you write—the more you practice, the better you'll get. And just as a violin player learns from listening to the music of professional violinists, you can learn a lot about writing from reading the works of good authors.

> *The more you read, the more you learn what you like and what you don't like. The more you write, the more your style develops.*

You may often see things you wish you had written and begin to get an idea of how you want to write. But recognizing good writing does not mean that you imitate it. Reading should influence you but not tell you what words to use. That has to come from within you, yourself.

This section is designed to help you develop the skills and discipline you need to write well. No matter what form, or genre, your writing takes, there are time-tested ways of expressing your ideas clearly and convincingly with words that the reader will appreciate and remember.

Writing Well Is a Skill

A beginning pianist has to master the scales and learn to recognize the notes in order to play music. In the same way, a beginning writer must understand grammar and basic techniques of writing well in order to build interesting stories, essays, and exciting reports.

The following tips on basic usage will keep your writing strong, clear, and bold. They're easy to understand and easy to use!

Build Sentences and Paragraphs

Sentences build on one another to create a paragraph that holds one idea, or, in the case of story writing, one phase of action. To make your writing strong and polished, start with the basics: the sentence and the paragraph.

A Sentence Consists of a Subject and a Verb

Jessica (subject) is not a sentence, but

Jessica sang. (subject + verb) is a sentence.

A Sentence Always Contains at Least One Thought

Jessica sang.

But a sentence can contain more than one thought:

At choir practice, Jessica sang and blinked back the tears as she thought of missing her favorite TV show.

(For more information about the grammar of the sentence, refer to Polishing Your Work, page 250.)

Start a New Paragraph with Each New Idea

In a story a new paragraph can mean a shift in action or time. In a report or an essay a new paragraph means that you are starting a new argument or idea. You show that you are beginning a new paragraph by indenting the first sentence of the new paragraph.

Suddenly and unexpectedly Jessica's father walked into the choir's practice room carrying a giant TV set!

You need another new paragraph when a different person is speaking.

"What on earth are you doing with the TV in here?" demanded Mrs. O'Connor.

And you need another one when the action switches back.

Without a word, Jessica's father plugged in the giant TV and tuned it to the channel so that Jessica could watch her beloved TV show.

Building Paragraphs Takes Careful Work

In a report or essay, the sentences within the paragraph develop the idea in its topic sentence.

> *Eating fast food is bad for you. It tastes good, but it is not healthful. Reports by consumer advocacy groups show that in many fast-food places basic standards of cleanliness are not being practiced. The levels of salt and fat in fast foods are extremely high. I interviewed many fast-food workers who said they don't even eat the food they make because they know <u>how</u> it's made. For me that was enough reason to stop eating fast food in a hurry.*

The topic sentence in the above paragraph is

> *Eating fast food is bad for you.*

The middle of the paragraph gives you reasons to support the writer's claim.

Reports by consumer advocacy groups show that in many fast-food places basic standards of cleanliness are not being practiced. The levels of salt and fat in fast foods are extremely high. I interviewed many fast-food workers who said they don't even eat the food they make because they know <u>how</u> it's made.

The final sentence concludes the ideas mentioned in the essay:

For me that was enough reason to stop eating fast food in a hurry.

Think of the Sentence and the Paragraph Together

A paragraph may consist of only a single sentence.

But none of the memories I have described is my favorite.

This could be a complete paragraph. A single-sentence paragraph can be a dramatic way of catching your reader's attention. However, because you have a lot to say, most paragraphs, like the following one, will have several sentences:

My favorite memory was the time my granddad and I went fishing. The weather was stormy but Poppa insisted we go anyway. We drove to the lake and boarded the rowboat. I was scared because the winds were gale force. Granddad remained stalwart. "This will make you strong," he told me, and only a half second later the wind blew him out of the boat, and he fell into the lake. I had to jump in to save him. It was hard to swim, but finally we made our way to the shore. "You're right," I said proudly. "This did make me strong."

Sometimes your work for an assignment will consist of a single paragraph. This is fine, but look over your writing and try to find a way to divide it into more than one paragraph. If it makes sense to do so, form several paragraphs. It's easier for the reader to read several small paragraphs than a single long paragraph.

> *My favorite memory was the time my granddad and I went fishing. The weather was stormy but Poppa insisted we go anyway. We drove to the lake and boarded the rowboat. I was scared because the winds were gale force. Granddad remained stalwart.*
>
> *"This will make you strong," he told me, and only a half second later the wind blew him out of the boat, and he fell into the lake. I had to jump in to save him. It was hard to swim, but finally we made our way to the shore.*
>
> *"You're right," I said proudly. "This did make me strong."*

Make a New Paragraph Each Time the Speaker Changes

Indenting the speech of characters in your stories or report makes clear who is saying what.

> *"I hear that snow is expected tomorrow," I said brightly.*
> *"Isn't that nice!" Dad replied.*
> *"All the more reason to do your chores now so that tomorrow you can play," interjected Mother.*

In Longer Writing, Use Paragraphs as Building Blocks

In the following story, John uses three paragraphs to help create a moving portrait of his grandmother.

> *It was always difficult to argue with Grandma, so I didn't bother and started picking currants as she had asked me to. Grandma told me that she used to pick currants with her father in Sea Cliff, Long Island, when she was a little*

*girl. She also told me about picking blueberries on the is-
lands of Elk Lake in the Adirondacks. I told Grandma that
I had picked raspberries along the trails at Elk Lake that
summer and those raspberries tasted better than any
others I had ever eaten. She smiled.*

*We continued to pick currants until the last bucket was
completely full. I asked Grandma why she was going to
make so much jelly. She said that she liked to give her
own jelly to her friends whenever she went to visit. I
helped her carry the buckets up to her house, but I never
saw her make the jelly. I fell asleep before she started.*

*The next morning there were rows of small jars of all
kinds and sizes filled with fresh jelly on the table next to
the stove. The biggest jar was labeled "For John. My best
picker. Love, Grandma." It was delicious.*

In paragraph one, John sets the scene for his memory:
His grandmother has asked him to pick currants with her
and, even though he doesn't want to, he does. While picking together, he and his grandmother swap stories about
berry picking.

In paragraph two, the picking is finished and John falls
asleep before he can help his grandma turn the currants
into jelly.

In paragraph three, John wakes to find the currants
transformed into jelly as if by magic and a lovely present
from his grandmother, thanking him for their time together.

Clarity Requires Discipline

Keep the Action in One Time Frame

When you are **telling** a story in conversation, you might
find that you often change tenses for a slangy effect.

> *I went to my mom, "Like, I need to eat some potato chips." And she goes, "Absolutely not!"*

> *I go to the dance and I'm standing there all alone when this friend of my brother's came up to me and asks me to dance!*

This is very lazy English when it is spoken. When it is written down and read, this switching of verb tenses is positively dizzying!

In this case, **asked** and **replied** are in the past tense:

> *I asked my mom, "May I have some potato chips?" And she <u>replied</u>, "Absolutely not!"*

and

> *I went to the dance. I was all alone when a friend of my brother's came up to me and <u>asked</u> me to dance.*

As a Rule, Stick to the Active Voice

The active, direct account is clearer than the passive, or "as told to," voice and much more lively. Which sentence makes you want to read more?

> *At the beginning of the novel, we are introduced to Gene as a shy and dependent person.*

or

> *Gene is shy and dependent at the beginning of the novel.*

By making the subject of the sentence the source of the action instead of the recipient of the action, you make the sentence itself bolder, more dramatic, and more interesting.

Use the Passive Voice to Emphasize the Action Rather Than the Subject

The sentence

Abraham Lincoln was assassinated.
(subject)   (passive verb)

emphasizes the fact that President Lincoln was assassinated.

Writing the same sentence with an active verb gives a different emphasis.

John Wilkes Booth   assassinated   Lincoln.
(subject)   (verb)   (object)

In the active sentence, the murderer is emphasized more than Lincoln himself.

Use Positive Forms Instead of Negative Ones

Clear writing is writing that says exactly what it means. For this reason, a positive statement, such as

Jasper **was ecstatic** when he joined Little League.

is stronger than the negative form:

Jasper **was not unhappy** when he joined Little League.

The negative form can be used to create a sarcastic or understated tone.

Harry **was not disappointed** when the teacher called on someone else.

Using the negative here suggests that you are stating the obvious in a sly, clever way. You should use it only occasionally for effect.

Put Up Signposts:
Punctuation and Headings

Punctuation and headings help guide readers through your words. Punctuation can make the difference in meaning between

We're going to the football game.

and

We're going to the football game?

and

We're going to the football game!

Punctuation can also help clarify a sentence that could otherwise be misunderstood. Notice the crucial role a comma plays in the following sentence.

Paul passed the popcorn to Alisa, and Jack, who had been waiting in the lobby, came into the theater and sat down.

Now read the same sentence without the comma and notice the confusion caused by its absence.

Paul passed the popcorn to Alisa and Jack, who had been waiting in the lobby, came into the theater and sat down.

Without the comma after Alisa, we would have thought that Paul has passed the popcorn to Alisa *and* Jack and then as we continued to read the rest of the sentence, we would have been thoroughly confused.

For a complete review of punctuation, go to Polishing Your Work, page 250.

Use Headings or Subtitles to Guide the Reader

Headings or subtitles keep the reader focused on what you have to say. They may also keep *you* focused on what you need to say. You can come up with titles for each paragraph you write by taking them from your outline. When you have finished writing, you may take the titles out or leave them in, depending on how much they add to the overall presentation.

Do you remember Ben's outline from page 215? This is how his report looked.

Madeleine L'Engle
Author — Doreen Gonzales

Madeleine L'Engle is a children's writer, a very good children's author. She loves her family (and still does). One day she decided to write a book called <u>A Wrinkle in Time.</u> Publishers turned it down. She finally told her agent that "the story is too peculiar. No one will ever publish it   "[1] Then, "one morning . . . Ruth Gagliardo told Madeleine that <u>A Wrinkle in Time</u> had won the 1963 Newbery Medal."[2] Madeleine had written for a long time. After nearly three decades of writing, . . . her . . . novel had won the Newbery Medal and she was very happy. (Wouldn't you be?)

Her Childhood

Madeleine was considered stupid as a child. Once, her poem won first prize in her school contest, and her teacher didn't believe she had written it. "Madeleine isn't bright . . . she must have copied it."[3] Her teacher also said she was "clumsy and dumb."[4] The teacher also held up Madeleine's papers and laughed at them in front of the class. Now Madeleine's "stupid" work is considered to be fine writing.

Madeleine was also very observant. Nobody guessed how keenly Madeleine observed things during family trips, not even her mother. Years later, Madeleine described them in detail.

Madeleine Today

Today, Madeleine lives in New York. She has three children and three grandchildren. She was married to Hugh Franklin, who was an actor. He died in 1986 of cancer. Madeleine (surprise, surprise!) wrote a book about their life together. Madeleine has written almost thirty books to date, and I hope she will continue.

Beware of the Run-on Sentence

Run-on sentences are two sentences joined together without punctuation or with just a comma. Here is one:

Odysseus left the Lotus Eaters, he visited the Cyclops and took a group of men into one of the many caves where they met a Cyclops who ate two men and went to sleep.

One simple way to correct this sentence is to substitute a period for a comma.

Odysseus left the Lotus Eaters. He visited the Cyclops and took a group of men into one of the many caves where they met a Cyclops who ate two men and went to sleep.

But you could turn the first part into a dependent clause.

After Odysseus left the Lotus Eaters, he visited the Cyclops and took a group of men into one of the many caves where they met a Cyclops who ate two men and went to sleep.

You might also break the passage into shorter sentences.

After Odysseus left the Lotus Eaters, he visited the Cyclops. He took a group of men into one of the many caves. There they met a Cyclops who ate two men and went to sleep.

Only you know which style works for you. The important thing is that every sentence has a complete thought with a subject and a verb.

Style suggestion:
Always try to get at the essence of what you have to say. It may take time to rewrite sentences, but they will be clearer and more readable when you do.

Variety Is the Spice of Life

In general, good writers use active verbs, short sentences, and positive statements. But there are exceptions to all these rules. You will sometimes want to use the passive voice or the negative form, and write long, winding sentences. Every style rule is made to be broken *occasionally* to keep the reader from getting bored. Take care not to break rules of grammar while you are at it! (For help with grammar, go to Polishing Your Work, page 250.)

Use a Thesaurus and a Dictionary

Writing gives you the chance to think in a formal way. You might find that you do not always have the right words to say what you mean. Use a thesaurus to enlarge your vocabulary. English is a colorful language with thousands of choices for describing things. For instance, a stream of water can be described as trickling, seeping, bubbling, babbling, racing, cascading, scampering, silent, rushing, gushing, or dancing, to name a few. Only *you* know which word best portrays the stream you have in mind. Maybe you'll find a word that you haven't thought about.

A dictionary is better than a thesaurus for making sure you are using a particular word correctly and that it is spelled right.

Every Genre Has a Style

Your writing style will vary with the kind of writing you do. Writing a report is very different from writing a story, so different rules of style apply. For example, you might write a story or play in which a character says,

"This is not very cool. I'm, like, really bored."

That may be considered good fictional writing, because it sounds like something that someone might actually say. But the same kind of style does not work when you write up your science experiment. The sentence

The liquid turned this really cool color.

would be poor writing. In writing about science, precision and observation are praised, not the way you use slang. The reader (perhaps your teacher) wants to know exactly what color the liquid turned—bright pink or pale blue.

Think About Your Audience

Another key question in choosing a style for an assignment is "Who will read this?" If you are writing a report that you will read to the entire class, you will want to write in such a way as to keep your classmates and your teacher interested. But if you are writing a report that only your teacher will read, your tone—and the content—may change. A movie review for the school newspaper will not have the same tone as a letter to your grandparents. Different readers want to know different things.

You might also think about the effect you want your writing to have on the reader. Do you want to entertain or inform? Do you want to move your audience to tears or spasms of laughter? Do you want to create an atmosphere of suspense? Or should the reader immediately volunteer to work on the cause you feel so passionately about? Whatever you intend, keep it in mind as you write.

Reports Give Information

When a Clear Explanation Is Required, Make Sure You Know the Answer First

A very common assignment is to explain something to the reader. You may be asked to show that you understand what you have read in a book or what you have done in a science experiment. Or you may be asked to research a topic in several sources and write a single report. Making an outline will help you decide what you really understand and what still seems unclear. You will have to find the answers for yourself before you can put them into writing. If you are vague, your writing will sound dull and confusing. No matter what fancy words you choose, they will never cover up a lack of understanding. Make the effort to get real answers. If your notes are unclear, return to the source until you understand exactly.

Good explanations are easily understood.
When you're satisfied that you have all the information you need, strive to be crystal clear in your writing. You'll show your teacher how much attention you paid, and your writing will make sense.

Again, a big key to writing well is taking the *time* to do so.

It may be easier to write

> *Sandy and I stood over the test tube. The test tube was on this thing called a Bunsen burner. Then I poured the purple stuff in. It smelled bad. That's when we noticed the vinegar had turned this sort of red color. Cool.*

But it's much better to read

> *Today's experiment was to discover what would happen when you add citric acid to vinegar while the vinegar was being heated.*
>
> *1. Sandy and I carefully placed our plastic goggles over our eyes and put on plastic gloves as a safety measure in the event of an accident with the chemicals.*
>
> *2. Sandy filled the test tube with four ounces of household vinegar.*
>
> *3. I slowly turned the gas switch on the Bunsen burner, struck a match, and lit the burner.*
>
> *4. Sandy used the tongs to place the test tube over the flame. The liquid began to bubble, which meant it had reached boiling temperature.*
>
> *5. I measured an ounce of citric acid, which was purple, and poured it into the vinegar.*
>
> *6. For a split second the mixture caught fire because of the reaction between the two chemicals. Then the flame went out, and what remained was a cherry-pink liquid—the brightest color I think I have ever seen.*

In the first passage, which is carelessly written, the reader does not know what Sandy and the writer are doing and certainly won't know why. In the second passage, the writer gives us the details. We know the purpose of the experiment and how it was conducted—step-by-step. With this report, we could repeat the experiment exactly as the students did it. Detail and clarity work together to make the writing strong.

Sources give you information, but the writing is up to you.
When you get information from a book or the Internet or by interviewing someone, you may take notes using the words of the source. Before you begin to write, you should read over the notes to make sure you understand them. Next, you demonstrate that you understand the information by putting the facts and ideas into your own words. (This is sometimes called paraphrasing.)

Footnotes Credit Sources

If you use someone else's words, put them in quotation marks and tell the reader who said them. In his report on the biography of Madeleine L'Engle, Ben used only one book but he placed quotation marks around the parts he copied directly and used little numbers to mark each one. Then, at the end, he listed the source. These are called footnotes, and you may use them to quote one, or several, sources.

Ben's footnotes for the report on Madeleine L'Engle's biography (see pages 225–226) looked like this:

> 1. Doreen Gonzales, *Madeleine L'Engle,* New York, Macmillan Publishing Co., 1991, p. 79.
>
> 2. Gonzales, p. 80.
>
> 3. Gonzales, p. 25.
>
> 4. Gonzales, p. 22.

If Ben had used more than one source, each one would have been listed just like his first footnote. In more academic reports, writers often use the Latin term op. cit., for a later reference to the same book, as in

> 2. *Gonzales, op. cit., p. 80.*

And if they quote the same book in the very next reference, they use

> 3. *Ibid., p. 4.*

Footnotes are only one way for crediting an author. For example, Ben might have written

> *One day she decided to write a book called <u>A Wrinkle in Time.</u> Publishers turned it down. She finally told her agent that "the story is too peculiar. No one will ever publish it. . . ." (Gonzales, p. 79)*

Paraphrase; Don't Plagiarize

The ideas and information of other people paraphrased and mixed with other sources throughout a report do not need direct quotations, but you should list all your sources in a separate bibliography. (See Presenting Your Work, page 267.)

Plagiarism means copying the ideas and words of others. Don't do it! It's worse than writing badly. It's cheating.

Don't Be Boring

You should make your readers feel that what you are reporting is interesting and important. The only way the reader will feel this is if you yourself find the subject interesting and important. If you are bored by a topic, look more closely to find at least one part that you find interesting. Emphasize what is interesting to you, and you will be sure to write convincingly about it. Furthermore, your report will be original.

Essays Show You Care

Essays Express Your Thoughts and Opinions

In a report, you work to explain information clearly and without an opinion. In an essay, you try to persuade the reader that your ideas are correct and meaningful. Whether your essay is about *Little Women,* nuclear waste, or pop music, you'll want your ideas to be clear and your writing to be engaging. A good tip to keep in mind is:

If your ideas don't make sense to you, they won't make sense to anyone else.

An outline or word clusters are useful when organizing an essay. (See Planning Your Work, page 208.) A strong essay should include about three arguments or ideas. It's better to develop a few ideas fully than to throw lots of half-baked notions at the reader. You won't make your essay better by having a long list of ideas.

Opening paragraphs should be strong.

In the opening paragraph of an essay, you want to grab the reader by the shirt collar and make her or him pay attention to what you've got to say. You do this by finding a first sentence that is direct, strong, and to the point. Ben had this to say about a novel he read:

> *In my opinion, the biggest conflict in <u>Lord of the Flies</u> was person versus person. The conflict of Ralph and Jack (good versus evil) dominated the story. It was one of the reasons Jack's tribe was against Ralph. The other reason was that Jack always wanted to be the best. In this essay I will further explain the central conflicts of <u>Lord of the Flies.</u>*

In the first paragraph you want to state the thrust of your essay and let the reader know what your opinions are. For the rest of the essay you will share with the reader good reasons why he or she should agree with you.

By the end of the first paragraph the reader should understand what you are writing about and should be interested enough to want to read more. The smooth and flowing style of your writing will make reading your essay a pleasure.

After you state your opinion, back it up.

In another book report, Ben does a good job of explaining his opinion.

> *What was unique about the gorilla part in* Congo *was that in most science-fiction novels, the author creates this whole, totally different reality. Everything in it is different. However, in* Congo, *a lot—actually everything—is the same except that he took a species of animal and gave it superior intelligence. He didn't make many major changes except that.*
>
> *I enjoyed the book a lot because it is believable and original. This is not true of most science-fiction books I've read.*

In a few sentences, we've learned that Ben liked this book and know why he did. In a good essay, the writer focuses his ideas around his thoughts and opinions, rather than the facts. That doesn't mean the facts don't count. You must understand and explain the facts if you want your opinion to sound informed.

Play devil's advocate: Try to disagree with yourself.

A devil's advocate is someone who preaches the opposite of what is believed to be right. Suppose your essay contains three ideas you're proud to say that you've thought up all by yourself. Test their mettle. Read over your essay and try to disagree with yourself.

If you wrote

> *Little Women is a good book. The character of Jo is the most interesting.*

ask yourself why Jo is the most interesting character to you. This may lead to your writing

> *Little Women is a good book with very interesting characters, but it was Jo that most caught my imagination because she is a tomboy and wants to be a writer.*

Or if you were writing

> *An advertisement for the nuclear energy industry claims that nuclear energy is the cleanest form of energy, but I disagree. It's amazing how people just ignore the dangers of nuclear waste.*

you could ask yourself why, if it's such a big problem, do people ignore it? While asking that question you might realize that not everyone ignores the problem of nuclear waste. You don't! And why is that? Then you might come up with something like this:

> *Nuclear waste is a big problem, but most people just ignore it. Maybe this is because they don't know much about it. I became interested in nuclear waste during my Environmental Science class. I learned that the waste created by burning nuclear fuel will be dangerous, even deadly, for many, many generations. That is why some people are concerned about whether there is any really safe place to dispose of nuclear waste. Perhaps if more people knew the dangers, they would demand that their power companies use other forms of energy or put more*

research into finding a way to burn nuclear fuels more efficiently with less waste.

Playing devil's advocate with your own writing enriches your ideas. You may even change your mind about something and come up with better, stronger opinions. At the very least, you will make your writing more interesting. It may take extra time—but it's worth it. The proof will be in your writing!

Beware of generalizations.

A **generalization** is a sweeping statement that is almost certainly not true—even though people tend to make generalizations with a very confident tone.

Some generalizations you may have heard, or even said, are:

90210 will always be my favorite show—even when I'm 80 years old.

Mexican food is always spicy and hot.

The Smiths, who live next door, are all alike.

Boys are obnoxious.

All girls love the color pink.

I hate vegetables.

I'll never wear fuchsia.

It feels very dramatic to say such exaggerated things—but they sound pretty silly (and can make you appear uninformed). Of course, *90210* will not be your favorite show throughout your life! And you can't really hate every single vegetable that ever sat on your plate—or those vegetables you have yet to try.

Say precisely what you think. It may sound less dramatic than a sweeping statement, but it will definitely carry more power.

Generalization:

90210 will always be my favorite show.

Precision:

Right now, 90210 is my favorite show.

Closing paragraphs pull it together.

In the closing paragraph of an essay, bring together all your ideas. The closing paragraph should complement the opening paragraph. You should be able to say in the final paragraph that you fulfilled the promises you made in your opening paragraph.

In the conclusion of this essay about *Tom Sawyer,* Lia sums up her ideas about the main character.

> *Tom does break rules and makes a lot of trouble, but there is more good to him than a lot of people think. He shows sympathy and kindness in most of his actions. It may take a lot of work to get the few words, "I love you," out of his mouth, but it is possible. When Tom lies to Aunt Polly about the dream he had, Aunt Polly cries over how much he doesn't care enough to show her respect. Tom replies, "Now auntie, you know I do care for you." He is always a good friend to Huck Finn, while nobody else pays attention to him. Tom may be mischievous, but at heart he is a good boy.*

You May Use the Poet's Tools

Creating Word Images Makes Your Writing More Vivid

When you write poetry, you want to be careful and precise with every word. There are several ways you can use words to make them create a mental picture for the writer. We call these word pictures imagery. While poets use imagery most often, it can also bring grace to your prose.

Use similes and metaphors to compare objects and ideas.
In a simile, you can compare something you are writing about with something else the reader will recognize.
　　Kwam writes

> *A plane dropped bombs <u>like</u> watermelons from the sky.*

Lia writes

> *That useless life did nothing, just sat around like a hanger with no coat.*

Metaphors are much like similes, but they do not use like or as.
　　Lia writes

> *Silence is the winter*
> *It is the snow*
> *Silence is the whiteness*

Crash! Bang! It's onomatopoeia.
Onomatopoeia uses words to imitate real sounds.
　　Lia writes

> *Milk, so ordinary, so plain*
> *But what would life be*
> *without milk*

> *Moooooooo! Yep, that's where*
> *it all starts*

And Ben writes

> *Wham! I hear as the ball hits*
> *the floor.*
> *Parents talking; kids yelling.*
> *The silent swish of the basket.*
> *Clank.*

Alliteration

The repetition of the same sound at the beginning of two or more words next to or near each other is called **alliteration.**

Lia writes

> *Come with me to the wet, windy, wond'rous land.*

Personification makes things "human."

Personification means giving human qualities to things that are not human.

Here, Ellen writes in the voice of a piece of bread being used in a sandwich.

> *The slice lay moaning as the finger crushed its center.*

And Cassidy writes

> *The water lily weeps*
> *and makes a pool for the tiniest bugs.*

Rhymes Are One of the Poet's Oldest Tools

Probably the first poems you heard were written in rhyme. Rhymes are formed by the vowel sounds at the end of words. A perfect rhyme is formed when words have the same end sound preceded by a different consonant.

Kwam writes

I think you're so humble
And you never mumble

And Lia writes

Down, down, down the stairs
Went the table and the chairs

These are perfect rhymes, but many people make rhymes with less than perfect sounds. For example, they might rhyme the words *charm* and *false alarm*. These are called slant rhymes and they are often used in songs and rap. For new ideas on words that rhyme, you might consult *The Scholastic Rhyming Dictionary*.

Rhyming patterns

Poets write rhymes in many patterns. Some of the simplest are the **couplet,** in which two lines rhyme, one after the other.

Jason writes

Willie Worm's home was an apple tree.
His family was content as worms can be.

In this rhyme scheme, every other line rhymes. It's called a,b,a,b.

Samantha writes

We're HOME ALONE, Hurray! Hurray!(a)
With no one to tell us, "Stop!"(b)
With junk food and some games to play(a)
We'll party 'til we drop.(b)

There are many other rhyme patterns, some of which can be very complicated. But you can have fun with rhymes without using a formal pattern, as Kwam does here.

When I grow up
I want to be an astronaut.
I want to fly
high
up in the sky,
into space,
First I'd go to Jupiter.
Then I'd go to Pluto.
Then I'd come back
to relax.

Verses Are the Paragraphs of Poetry

Poems are written in **verses**, rather than paragraphs. But as with prose, the writer shapes each verse around a single idea.

Katherine writes

I am sheltered.
When I walk out of my house,
I am not stepping into a society
of violence.
I am not like others who live in an
environment
where kids carry guns just for
protection
to walk to school.

In another verse, she writes

I am sheltered.
I do not wake up in the morning
wondering if I will have food to eat.
Without a thought, I go downstairs to
grab a snack
while some children are starving.

At the conclusion of her poem, she sums up her thoughts:

> *I take so many things for granted.*
> *I cannot even comprehend*
> *what life is like for some of*
> *these people.*
> *We are all living in the same world,*
> *yet we all view it differently.*
> *I hear about the ugliness of the*
> *world, but I do not see it.*
> *I hear about hate, violence,*
> *starvation, war, poverty,*
> *but it is not happening to me.*
> *I am secure in my surroundings*
> *where I am kept innocent and*
> *ignorant,*
> *Ignorant of what the world is like*
> *for the ones who are suffering.*
> *I am sheltered.*

Fiction Is a Figment of the Imagination

When you write fiction, the story is yours to shape. The people in your fiction, the characters, may be entirely made-up, or they may be based on real people. The place, or setting, in which the story takes place may be down the street—or in another galaxy. It's up to you. The idea is to create a believable situation in which your story can take place. Since you create the characters and the setting, it's up to you to make sure that they make sense to the reader. If your story takes place on a desert island, the main character will not be able to call out for pizza. You create a situation or problem that is the crux of your story. Then you tell the story in such a way that builds to a climax and that has your readers eager to hear what is going to happen. Finally, you bring all the pieces together in the end, which is often called the **resolution**. The story can be one page long or many chapters. It's all up to you.

In this story, the leading character, or **protagonist**, is a girl. Cassidy begins

> *My best friend Alice was moving away. Okay, so I was feeling a little glum. But hey, isn't everybody? I mean it's not every day that your lifelong companion is moving away forever. You can't exactly celebrate the moment, can you?*
>
> *Let me begin at the beginning.*

Next, Cassidy tells us a bit about the protagonist.

> *I know, I know. Whiny opening, huh? My name is Amanda Wikstaff. I'm twelve years old. I have short blond hair, a slender figure, and chocolate-brown eyes. My nose is very short. Too short. I keep pulling at it but nothing ever happens.*

Now that we know a little bit about Amanda, we meet her family.

> *Mom says I'm a little small for my age. In other words, I'm a shrimp. But I don't care. My ten-year-old brother Doug always calls me Tubs. I don't know why. I'm very skinny for my age. But I guess it's just his way of showing he doesn't know anything.*

And skillfully, Cassidy moves back to the character's problem.

> *Anyway, my best friend is moving away and there is nothing I can do about it. My mom said, "You'll always find new friends."*

> *I screamed at her, "That's what you think!" Then I ran up to my room and slammed the door.*

Before long, Amanda has jumped on her bike and pedaled over to Alice's house for one last good-bye. Instead, she finds a FOR RENT sign on the door. Here's what happens next.

> *With a defeated sigh, I sank to the ground. I let out a low moan. Not only would I never see her again, but I didn't even get to say good-bye either!*
>
> *Suddenly, someone tapped me on the shoulder. I stared into the face of a hideous monster. Green globs dripped from its snoutlike nose. Blood-spattered fangs opened and shut. Ants were strewn in the green monster's hair. I stared wide-eyed into the creature's blue eyes, and suddenly, I recognized them.*
>
> *"Doug!" I roared, "you jerk!"*

As it turns out, Doug is wearing a mask. Furious, Amanda then pedals back home and phones another girl, Katy. She invites her for a sleepover.

> *Later that night, snickering softly to ourselves, Katy and I made our way back to my room and opened my closet door. I lay on the floor with my head and arms half hidden inside the closet and only my legs and slippers showing. Then I closed my eyes and waited while Katy woke Doug. A few seconds later, Doug entered my room. When he saw me sprawled out on the floor, he gave a shriek of terror and ran to my parents' room. We chuckled to ourselves. It had worked. He had run from terror. Pure terror. Now Doug and I were even.*

Amanda's parents wake up and tell everybody to settle down, and they go to sleep. Here's how Cassidy ends her story.

The next morning, I swigged a glass of orange juice and gulped down my cornflakes. Then I ran a brush through my short blond hair. I grabbed my windbreaker and ran outside. Then I slipped on my Rollerblades and skated with Katy to her house. The sun felt good on my face. Katy and I were good friends now that Alice was gone. Before, all three of us, Katy, Alice, and I, had been known as the gruesome threesome. And now we would be known as the gruesome twosome.

Although the fiction writer is creating a story, many of the stylistic devices that make any writing smooth are put to good use. Cassidy tells her story in short, crisp sentences. She uses the active voice (see page 222) and allows the characters to speak in carefully punctuated dialogue. Her sentences build to paragraphs that have a beginning, a middle, and an end—just as her story does.

You may notice that Amanda usually speaks in a certain tone. Whenever we read it, we know she is speaking.

I know, I know. Whiny opening. . . . Anyway, my best friend is moving away and there is nothing I can do about it. Not only would I never see her again, but I didn't even get to say good-bye either!

Your Script Can Put Words into People's Mouths

Most writers assume that the words they write will be read or listened to exactly as they express them. But writers who want their work produced onstage or in movies or on television write in a different style. A script contains words that will be spoken. Other parts of the writer's work are invisible to the audience—but necessary to the story.

Scripts Have a Special Format

Scripts for plays or films follow a different form from other writing. Part of a script is **dialogue**, which the characters will speak. But a scriptwriter must also be concerned with giving other people—producers, directors, actors, makeup experts and wardrobe people, light and (sometimes) camera crews—instructions for the overall effect the play should create.

Some of the other parts of the script include:

- **the cast:** a list of all the characters with descriptions of those people.

- **the setting:** a detailed description of where each part of the script takes place.

- **stage instructions:** where the actors should be when they speak to each other on stage, how they speak, what they should do.

- **the prologue:** what the writer wants the audience to know about what it is going to hear and see.

- **the epilogue:** action that takes place after the story shown in the play or film is completed, or the writer's thoughts about the meaning of the play.

You Need a Cast

A script begins with a list of all the characters who will appear. In this script for television, Amanda lists her characters with a brief description of each.

> **Mike's Grandfather:** He owned the house that Mike's parents have kept up these past years. He disappeared about seven years ago, and by now all have given up hope of ever finding him.

Mike: He is a teenager with a passion for adventure. He is very athletic. He does not take great responsibility well, though.

Joe: He is another teenager who is very intelligent and knows how to take charge in stressful situations.

Ashley: She is fifteen, the same age as Mike and Joe. She is very quiet and smart and able to assess strange situations.

Breanne: She is a very talkative girl and is very obsessed with her looks.

The Phantom: He is a faceless man who is the definition of evil. To him it matters little whom he hurts as long as he gets what he wants.

If you were a director or an actor looking for a part, reading the list of characters would be a big help to you. If you see a stage play, you will probably find this list in your program, but if you watch this play on television or in a movie, chances are you won't see this list until the credits roll at the end.

Plays Are Organized by Acts and Scenes

In a brief script, all the action can frequently be contained within one act. But in a longer script, the action may be broken into acts and scenes, just as books are broken into chapters and paragraphs. New acts and new scenes give the crew time to change scenery and actors the opportunity to change costumes.

In Scene 1 of her play's first act, Amanda gives only brief staging directions.

Act 1: Scene 1

[The time is seven years ago. Today Mike's grandfather enters the attic. Outside, lightning flashes. Mike's grandfather makes his way through the dusty clutter until he comes to a splendid Victorian full-length mirror. The mirror appears to be glowing. Lightning flashes again, and Mike's grandfather is gone.]

Notice that Amanda put these directions inside brackets. That signals to the reader that the words are not being spoken.

Settings tell where the writer envisions the action taking place.

In Scene 2 of Amanda's script, the action moves to another setting. Again, she gives the reader the information in brackets.

[We see a street in a current-day Massachusetts town. The houses along the street are old Victorian ones. You look farther down the street and see four kids riding their bikes. The sky is dark, and thunder can be heard in the distance.]

Notice how Amanda uses the setting to succinctly describe modern times while using the decrepit buildings and the weather to signal that something bad could be happening any minute.

Dialogue moves the action along.

As the characters begin to speak, the action starts rolling.

Mike [shouts]: Ashley, Breanne, would you two hurry up! I'd like to get to my grandpa's before this storm sets in!
Joe: Those two are so slow. [The girls catch up with them.]

*Ashley [offended]: Are not. We're better than you guys
    are at a lot of things.*
Breanne: Hey, like, where are we going, again?
*Joe [sounding quite annoyed]: For the millionth time, we
    are going to Mike's grandpa's house. Got it?*

Each act tells a part of the story.
Amanda's play continues for three acts. Many things happen before Mike's grandfather is rescued from the mirror where he is trapped. The script closes with shattered glass on the floor—and the image of the phantom still reflected.

Take a Break

Whew! You finally put your ideas onto paper. No matter what you produced—a report, an essay, a story, a poem, or a play—it's time to step away. Go for a walk, play with the dog, or call a friend. If you've given yourself enough time, you may want to wait until tomorrow to look at your work again. If you have less time, do something else—your math homework, for example—to clear your head before you begin the next step, polishing your writing.

Polishing Your Work

Fine-tuning

If you want to make your best impression—and a good grade—you're not finished. Look for things you may have missed when you were concentrating on organizing your ideas. Your excellent thoughts have to be presented in a way that makes sense to others. You can do this by using good grammar, punctuating clearly, spelling correctly, and editing critically.

Good grammar makes a good impression.

The basis for clear writing is good grammar. These are the rules by which everyone is guided—like rules in a soccer game. Although grammar changes slightly across the English-speaking world, there are standards for American English that you need to learn. Grammar helps you communicate your thoughts clearly. Incorrect grammar is a distraction. You impress others by showing that you know the rules and can follow them.

Check the Grammar of the Sentence

See pages 2–73 for grammar rules.

Punctuation Holds It All Together

Punctuation tells the reader how you want your words to be read. When you speak, your voice puts in many of these punctuation marks.

At the end of a sentence, you take a breath.
(You've just put in a period.)

When you ask a question, you raise your voice at the end.

(Does the listener hear a question mark?)

When you want to emphasize something, you say it louder.

(This is a doggone exclamation mark!)

When you pause during a sentence, you are deliberately separating certain words for clearer meaning.

(You, my friend, have just used a comma.)

When people are reading what you wrote, they have nothing to go by except the words they see on the paper. Punctuation takes the place of your voice.

Sentences Have to Begin and End

A sentence is a group of words that tell a complete thought. You signal the beginning of a sentence by capitalizing the first word and following the last word with a period, question mark, or exclamation mark. You can't expect the reader to know when you have finished one thought and gone on to another unless you mark each sentence.

If you wrote a paragraph without punctuating, it might look like this:

> *Every summer we go to a great camp in the mountains we go swimming sailing and fishing in the lake the first day of our vacation last summer I caught a huge trout reeling it in was exhausting and exciting I will never forget that day or the fish fry that followed.*

Without punctuation, the reader sees a jumble of words. With punctuation, it looks like this:

Every summer we go to a great camp in the mountains. We go swimming, sailing, and fishing in the lake. The first day of our vacation last summer I caught a huge trout. Reeling it in was exhausting and exciting. I will never forget that day or the fish fry that followed.

The reader has to be signaled about stops and pauses in order to understand the words.

See pages 76–103 for punctuation rules.

Standard Spelling Makes It Readable

Words are spelled the way they are because that spelling is traditional and is understandable to most Americans. Standard spelling assures the reader that your words can be trusted. Every day, however, we see words that have a shorthand or unconventional spelling.

Examples:

Ped Xing	pedestrian crossing
no thru way	not a through way
Xmas	Christmas
OK	okay
For Sale	for sale

Usually these words have been shortened because the abbreviated version takes up less space. Even though you understand these words, they should not be used in formal writing. Don't be tempted to take shortcuts.

When you read a book published in Canada or England, the spelling may be different. The same is true of books published a long time ago in the United States. If you don't know the modern American spelling for a word, look it up in a dictionary or run it through your computer spell check.

See pages 106–124 for spelling rules.

Watch for Confusing Words and Phrases

There are rules about the use of all words and phrases. Sometimes people either don't know these rules or they choose to ignore them. When words are misused over and over, often the wrong forms are so common that they become more and more acceptable—especially in everyday speech.

When writing, however, you need to know what is correct. Words that you misuse in talking with friends may look sloppy on paper.

Following are a few of the most commonly misused words. They are divided into four sections: Verbs, Prepositions, Adjectives and Adverbs, and Pronouns.

Some Verbs Are Tricky

Verbs are words that show action or a state of being. There are regular and irregular verbs. When learning to talk, small children usually make all verbs regular. They will say:

He **throwed** the ball.

My bike **runned** into the curb.

Uncle Jack **catched** my cold.

This pattern is certainly logical if all verbs were regular. With correction and experience, however, we learn that there are some verbs with irregular forms.

He **threw** the ball.

My bike **ran** into the curb.

Uncle Jack **caught** my cold.

(For more information about regular and irregular verbs, see Verbs, page 28.)

can – may

These two verbs are often used interchangeably. Although the listener seldom has trouble figuring out what is meant, you should use them precisely when you write.

Can means to be able.

May means to have permission.

Examples:

> May I climb that mountain?
> *(Do I have permission?)*

> Can I climb that mountain?
> *(Am I able?)*

could of – would of

These forms are incorrect. They began as *could have* and *would have,* shortened to the contractions *could've* and *would've,* which sounded like *could of* and *would of.* When writing, it is important to use the correct form.

Example:

> **Wrong:** He could of done it.

> **Right:** He could have done it.

or

> He could've done it.

goes – says

We often hear people say something like this:

I go, "Are you sure?" and he goes, "Sure," and I go, "Cool."

To go has many meanings, but it should not be substituted for *to say* or *to ask* or *to reply* or *to answer.* Instead, write

I **asked,** "Are you sure?" and he **replied,** "Sure." I **said,** "Cool."

Bonus: Here are some acceptable substitutions for **said.**

replied	whispered	answered
asked	commented	inquired
shouted	murmured	demanded

wait on – wait for

To **wait on** means to serve someone.

Example:

He **waited** on our table first.

To **wait for** means to stay put until something expected happens.

Example:

John **waited for** Teresa to come.
(John stayed put expecting Teresa to come.)

Note: Remember that at restaurants you wait for someone to wait on you.

Prepositions Make the Right Connections

Prepositions are words that connect ideas. There are about fifty prepositions in everyday use. The following are some that are frequently misused.

about – at about

About is sufficient by itself. At about is unnecessary.

Too wordy: We will eat at about one o'clock.

Better: We will eat about one o'clock.

among – between

Today between is used more often than among. The distinction between the two words is fading fast. However, there is a difference.

Between is a preposition used when there are two people, two things, or two groups.

Example:

Draw a line between the two points.

Among is a preposition meant to be used when there are more than two of something.

Example:

Choose one figure from among the triangle, the quadrangle, the circle, and the hexagon.

like – as

Like is a preposition that is followed by a phrase.

Example:

She snorts like a horse.

As is a conjunction. It introduces clauses with a subject and a verb.

Example:

Do as I do and not as I say.

in – into

In means inside something.

Into means moving toward something or moving inside it. Compare the following:

> Jack's pet canary flew in the house.

> Jack's pet canary flew into the house. (Ouch!)

For more information, see Prepositions, page 49.

Adjectives and Adverbs Should Be Precise

An adjective describes a noun or pronoun; an adverb describes a verb, adjective, or other adverb.

Example:

> The unhappy dog is barking loudly.

Unhappy is an adjective describing dog (a noun).

Loudly is an adverb describing barking (a verb).

Here are a few adjectives and adverbs that cause confusion:

anyway – anyways

The adverb anyway means in any case, anyhow. Anyway does not have a plural form. Therefore, anyways is never correct.

> **Wrong:** That's not the theme of the story anyways.

> **Right:** That's not the theme of the story anyway.

bad – badly

These two words are often confused. Bad is an adjective; badly is an adverb.

With parts of the verb to be—be, am, is, are, was, were, been—and with verbs relating to the senses—seem, look, feel, taste, sound, and smell—use the adjective bad.

Example:

> All the reviews of this movie were bad.

With an action verb, use the adverb badly.

Example:

> He left the cast of the play because he was performing badly.

fewer – less

Both fewer and less are used for comparisons. The difference is as follows:

Fewer refers to a smaller number of things.

Less refers to a smaller portion of one thing.

Examples:

> We have fewer assignments on weekends than on weekdays.

> We have less homework on weekends than on weekdays.

healthy – healthful

These two adjectives are used interchangeably, but there is a difference.

Healthy means to have good health.

Healthful means to give good health.

Examples:

> Regular exercise is healthful.

> To be healthy, exercise regularly.

most – almost

It is common to hear almost shortened to most. There is a difference.

Most means the greatest amount.

Almost means nearly.

Examples:

> Most cultures showed mold.

> Almost all of the cultures showed mold.

off – off of

Although you may hear off of a great deal, the of is unnecessary. Off is fine by itself.

> Unnecessary: Pablo risks his life by jumping off of a roof.

> Better: Pablo risks his life by jumping off a roof.

real – really

Real is often used when really is what is meant. They are different in meaning.

Real is an adjective that means true or actual.

Really is an adverb that means extremely.

Examples:

> A real story is often stranger than fiction.

What happened to him is really frightening.

You need an adverb to describe the adjective frightening.

See page 276 for 100 Easily Confused and Misused Words.

Substitute Pronouns with Care

Pronouns take the place of nouns. Confusion often results from not understanding which nouns they replace.

each other – one another

These words are used interchangeably. To be exact, however, each other refers to two people, and one another refers to three or more.

Examples:

Jerry and Cameron took turns questioning each other.

The team members shared ideas with one another.

himself – herself – themselves

Pronouns that end in self—myself, yourself, himself, herself, ourselves, yourselves, themselves—must match the noun or pronoun they make stronger or reflect.

Examples:

The queen herself never married.

When the battle was done, the knight and his squire congratulated themselves.

Hisself and theirselves are not words. They should never be used instead of himself and themselves.

Pronouns ending in **self** cannot be the subject of a sentence. **Myself** cannot be used instead of **I**.

Examples:

> **Wrong:** The teacher and **myself** were alone in the room.

> **Right:** The teacher and **I** were alone in the room.

its – it's

These words sound exactly alike, so they don't present a problem when you are speaking. When writing, however, you must differentiate.

Its is a possessive pronoun. Even though it shows possession, it does not have an apostrophe.

Example: My snake lost **its** skin.

It's is the contraction for **it is**. The apostrophe shows that the i is left out of the word **is**.

Example:

> I don't care if **it's** (it is) late.

who – that

Current usage is as follows:

Who refers to people.

> The blond girl is the one **who** spoke.

That may refer to both people and things.

> It was the dripping faucet **that** drove him crazy.

> The blond girl was the one **that** spoke.

Editing Makes It Shine

You may have heard that you never get a second chance to make a good first impression. That may be true with many things but not with writing. When you speak, your words jump out of your mouth and are gone. When you write, you have a second chance. You can even have third and fourth chances if you want them. Be sure you leave enough time to go over your work and make changes before you turn it in. Reviewing and changing what you have written is a valuable tool in developing writing style.

This One's for Your Eyes Only

Read your first draft straight through from beginning to end with the knowledge that you're going to rewrite and improve it. As you read it a second and even a third time, look at your words from the reader's point of view. Ask yourself:

- How do these words sound? Is the emphasis where I want it?

- Would a different word make the idea clearer?

- Am I repeating a certain word too much?

- Does the punctuation make it clear where to stop, to being, to pause?

Little Things Mean a Lot

As you read what you wrote, you will see ways to improve it. These may include:

- substituting a better word here and there.

- adding a word that may have been left out.

- crossing out unnecessary words.

- removing unneeded sentences.

- rewriting a sentence.

- combining paragraphs or dividing a paragraph.

- adding information or deleting off-target information.

- improving punctuation.

- changing paragraph order.

It's Not in Stone

Lots of writers like to think their first draft is their best. They are usually mistaken—or lazy. The best writers fine-tune their work long after the initial inspiration has passed. You may want to reshuffle pages or even cut them up and tape them together in new ways. Try reading to a friend or parent or, if you're by yourself, simply read aloud. If you read every word, you may be surprised by what you hear.

Computers Are Wonderful—Up to a Point

If you are using a word processor, it probably has many tools to help you edit.

Deleting
You can delete a word or phrase with a stroke of the keyboard, but ask yourself: Did I really want to delete those words? Did I delete only the words I meant to? Does deleting these words change the grammar of the sentence? Does it require me to change other words in the sentence?

Spell checking

It's often easy to misspell a word—even if you know how to spell it—in the rush to get your ideas into words. You should *never* turn in an assignment without running a spell check if you have one. But computers are machines. A spell check cannot detect a misspelled word if the spelling is correct for another word.

Example:

The nights eight and drank at there fast.

What you probably meant to write was:

The knights ate and drank at their feast.

The spell checker can't distinguish between **nights** and **knights**, **eight** and **ate**, **there** and **their**, and **fast** and **feast**—as long as each is spelled correctly.

Proper nouns present problems for most spell checkers, too. Not surprisingly, your computer will probably be stymied by Syracuse or Dred Scott. Some spell checkers have a feature that allows you to add words to your dictionary, so you may want to add proper nouns that you use frequently—after you check your dictionary or source to make sure you've spelled them correctly.

Moving text

Have you ever wondered how a piece of work would read if you put the last paragraph first or exchanged two sentences? With a word processor, this is a simple procedure. However, once you have moved the text and saved it, be sure you read your draft through again. It may not read as clearly as you expected. That is why Undo is a favorite command of many writers.

Grammar check

More recent word-processing programs have features that allow you to check basic grammar, such as subject-verb agreement and punctuation. A feature like this can be useful if you use it carefully. But make sure that you didn't punctuate oddly for effect, or bad grammar has not been used intentionally.

The Final Draft Is Done

Here is an example of a paragraph that was written, then reread and changed, and then put in final form:

First Draft:

> My grandmother is really nice to me, but she has to be really, really old. I mean, she is my mother's mother, and my mother is ancient. But when I am with my grandmother, we always have a good time. We do neat things like play the piano, go for walks, talk about how great I am, buy me presents, cook my favorite foods, and play games that I win. Maybe being really, really old isn't so bad when you have a really neat granddaughter like me.

Second Draft with changes and corrections:

> My grandmother is very nice, but she has to be really old. After all, she is my mother's mother, and my mother's ancient. When I'm with her, however, I always have a good time. We play the piano, go for walks, talk about how wonderful I am, buy me presents, cook my favorite foods, and play games that I always win. Maybe being so old isn't that bad when you have a terrific granddaughter like me.

Hard Work Pays Off

The advantage of reviewing and changing your work is that the finished product more closely says what you want. The final product shows none of these revisions. Because the material has been reviewed and revised, it reads more smoothly, is easier to understand, and reflects your thoughts more accurately. To the rest of the world, your final draft might well be your first draft. Only you know for sure.

Presenting Your Work

Your Best Paper Forward

Congratulations—you're finished! Well, almost finished. You can do a find job of planning, producing, and polishing your work and still make a bad impression on the reader if your presentation is sloppy.

Readers react not only to what is written but also to how it looks. A report, no matter how brilliant, must look as good as it really is.

If you want an A-plus, it must look like an A-plus paper.

Always make sure your paper is clean—no cola stains or ragged edges—and well labeled. You're not one of those people who forgets to include your name on the front page, are you?

The style of your presentation may vary. However, just as there are basics for writing well, there are basics for ensuring that material will make a positive impression under any conditions.

By Hand or Machine?

By now, you know how you will create your final draft. Will you write it, type it, or use a word processor? Each has its own rules.

Handwriting Can Be Impressive

Although few people make the effort to present them well anymore, handwritten reports can be elegant, impressive, and an expression of the writer's creativity. Start with a pen with plenty of ink. Blue-black is the most readable on white paper.

Find a smooth, uncluttered surface and give yourself time to write legibly. Select fresh, unwrinkled paper with clean edges. Before you begin, decide where you will put your margins—on the right and left and top and bottom—and stick with them. The lines can help guide you.

A little white correction fluid is permissible, but if you use it, make sure you let it dry before you write over it. If you make a lot of mistakes, it's better to start a new page.

Since your final draft has been carefully edited, stick to it.

Word Processors Are Nifty

If you use a word processor, no one has to tell you how handy it is for writing and rewriting. You may have already saved several versions of your writing. Now you can create your final paper without much effort.

Not so fast! In spite of the ease with which word processors make it possible for writers to create and save their work, some of the sloppiest presentations are electronically created. Why is this? Perhaps it's because people expect the machines to do all the work. No matter how powerful your computer, you, the writer, are in command. And if you skip some steps along the way, don't be surprised if your grades reflect it.

No computer can save you if you fail to use the special features of your word processor to create even margins, tabs, and spacing. It's up to you to enter the words carefully and to reread what you write.

Special print features

When you handwrite a report, you learn to underline words that should be in italics or boldface. Word processors can help you by actually creating italics and boldface type. Make sure you use these features consistently, not italicizing some titles and underlining others.

Most word processors give you a choice of print faces and sizes. If you are creating a manuscript in which there are examples or mathematical equations, these special features can help you lead the reader through your work.

When used wisely, a word processor and printer can help you look like a professional publisher. When used carelessly, they create the wrong impression.

Presentation Makes It Neat

Format Uniformly

The way you present your paper is called its format. It is the form you give your paper. For instance, the first time you indent a paragraph, you announce that this is how all paragraphs will be done.

Just as you are frustrated when playing a game with someone who changes the rules all the time, so readers are frustrated if you suddenly change your format. When you start writing, you are saying to the reader, "This is the way I'm going to do this." If you do something else, you have changed the rules. Be consistent.

Here are examples of common format decisions you should make:

- How big will your margins be? On either side? At top and bottom?

- Will paragraphs be indented or written in block form with extra space between paragraphs?

- How will you treat titles, heading, subheadings?

- Will you use abbreviations? If you do, be sure to abbreviate the same way every time. (For example, Atlanta, GA every time—never Atlanta, Georgia, then Atlanta, GA.)

- Will you spell out numbers over 100? (You should always write out numbers under 100.)

- Will you hyphenate words when they don't fit on a single line, or will you move the entire word to the next line?

- Will you use titles with people's names (Mr. Miss, Ms. or Mrs. Johnson, for example)?

- Will you use first names? Nicknames? Middle initials?

To a reader, a predictable, orderly format is like a security blanket.

Use Spacing to Organize Your Work

Well-spaced writing is easier to read and to understand. It looks organized. Here are some spacing suggestions that will improve your final presentation:

- Leave uniform space at the top and bottom of the page.

- Allow for a left and right margin of about one inch on each page.

- Keep the left margin straight and the right margin as uniform as possible.

- Allow extra space between paragraphs.

- Leave space above and below titles and headings.

- Double-space typed text.

- Give special attention to lines of poetry; spacing is often part of the poem.

- In scripts, lines of dialogue are often single-spaced with double-spacing between the speakers.

- Indent quoted passages from other works on both sides. These passages may be single-spaced.

- Use only one side of the paper unless instructed to do otherwise.

Spacing not only improves the look of your writing, it also makes it easier to read and, therefore, to understand.

Organize by Numbering

Pages

One of the most important ways to help readers is by numbering the pages. Anything over one page of writing should be numbered at the top center, the bottom, or the top right of each page. The numbers should appear in the same place on every page. By numbering the pages, you make it easier to find a certain page and to keep them in order. Some writers do not number the first page. If you follow this style, be sure the second page is numbered "2."

Sections

Divide your long works into sections and number them. If you use an outline to create a report, the Roman numeral headings often give you clues for section headings. If you write a long work of fiction, you may want to divide it into numbered chapters. Plays may be numbered by acts and scenes. (See page 247.)

The Table of Contents Goes Up Front

At the front of a long work, include a table of contents. Be sure to include the titles, your introduction, the bibliography, and any illustrations—and the number of the page on which each can be found.

Bibliographies Back It Up

When you began taking notes for your report or essay, you took careful notes about where you got your information, didn't you? (If you didn't, there's still time to return to the library.) All this material can now be organized at the back of your paper.

See page 204 for ways to format a bibliography.

Make That Final Check

Especially if you rewrote or retyped your final text, read your work out loud. If you can find a partner, this works even better. Reading aloud helps you to catch words that were dropped and words that were repeated. Your partner can also alert you to passages that are unclear or weak.

Reconsider Your Titles

When you started this writing project, you may have had a topic in mind. Maybe your teacher even suggested one. Now that you have written, revised, and polished your work, is the title appropriate? Or if the topic is essentially the same, would you like your title to be livelier? Now's your chance to call your work whatever you like. After all, you created it.

If your writing is serious, you need a serious title, but it doesn't have to be dull. *Abigail Adams* might become *Abigail Adams, Second First Lady,* or *Abigail Adams, Founding Wife and Mother.* Some writers like mysterious titles: *What I Found at the Mall* or, if you like to play around with sounds, *Mall Mice.* Poets and fiction writers often use single-word titles: *Fragments* or *Censored.* Titling your work is not unlike naming a pet. You want people to notice it and think you made a good choice.

Proofread

Before turning in your work, proofread it. Proofreading is different from reviewing a draft. When you review, you think of the content of what you wrote and how it sounds. When you proofread, you watch for grammatical and spelling errors. Check anything that looks odd by using this book or a dictionary. Make sure that every sentence is properly punctuated.

Look for careless errors—mistypings, misspellings, misnumberings, or format irregularities. These mechanical errors greatly affect how easily your final product can be read. These errors cause a reader to slow down and correct them mentally before being able to continue. They are like road bumps on an otherwise smooth street.

Give Yourself a Pat on the Back

Now that you've turned in your work, perhaps you can remember when it began—with only a topic and a few ideas. Now it's time to congratulate yourself. You're not just a person who puts any old thing on paper, but a careful, style-conscious writer. Producing good writing is probably a lot harder than you imagined, but it has its rewards. Among them may be not just good grades but a sense of pride and a little attention.

Part 7
General Reference

100 Easily Confused and Misused Words

In English some words sound and look very much like other words. They can be easily confused and misused. Here are 100 of the trickiest of these words.

n. = noun	**v.** = verb	**adj.** = adjective	
adv. = adverb	**pron.** = pronoun	**conj.** = conjunction	

accent, *n.* a manner of speech characteristic of a certain city, country, or region
ascent, *n.* the act of going up
In a French accent he told about his ascent of the mountain.

accept, *v.* to take what is offered or given
except, *prep.* leaving out; other than
They will accept everyone into the club except him.

adapt, *adj.* to change or adjust to a different situation
adept, *adj.* very skilled; expert in something
adopt, *v.* choose an idea to follow as one's own
He's not adept when he has to adopt new ideas or adapt to new situations.

affect, *v.* to influence, to change
effect, *n.* a result, a consequence
The student government hopes this meeting will affect (change) school rules. We think our suggestions will have a good **effect** (result) on student life.

alley, *n.* a narrow street or passageway
ally, *n.* a person or country united with another for a common purpose
Follow him quickly! He ducked down the alley with his closest ally.

all ready, everyone or everything is prepared
already, *adv.* previously; before this time; by this time
We were all ready for the class trip, but the bus had already left.

allusion, *n.* a mention or suggestion made indirectly or in passing
illusion, *n.* a false or misleading idea or belief; an unreal image
Are you making an allusion to The Wizard of Oz with your red shoes, or is it just an illusion?

altogether, *adv.* completely; in all
all together, at the same time; in the same place

*The conductor was **altogether** disgusted when the orchestra couldn't play the notes **all together**.*

anecdote, *n.* a short account of an incident or event
antidote, *n.* a remedy that counteracts the effects of poison
*She told me an **anecdote** about the time she used her grandmother's **antidote** when she was bitten by a poisonous snake.*

angel, *n.* an immortal, spiritual being; a very wonderful person
angle, *n.* the space between two lines that meet
*Be an **angel** and help me measure this **angle**.*

anyway, *adv.* in any case; at least
any way, in any manner
Anyway, my teacher told me to do the homework any way I knew how.

bibliography, *n.* a list of books or articles on a particular subject
biography, *n.* an account of a person's life
*On our **bibliography** of heroines, we should include the **biography** of Mother Teresa.*

breath, *n.* air that is taken into the lungs and let out again
breathe, *v.* to take air into the lungs and let it out again
*With each **breath** you take in the country, you **breathe** fresh air.*

cease, *v.* to put an end to; to stop

seize, *v.* to take hold of suddenly and forcibly
*Either **cease** those actions or I'll order the guards to **seize** you.*

coma, *n.* a state of deep unconsciousness caused by disease or injury
comma, *n.* a punctuation mark
*My English teacher practically goes into a **coma** when someone leaves out a **comma**.*

command, *v.* to order; to direct; to be in control
commend, *v.* to speak highly of; to praise
*If you're brave enough to **command** those wild three year olds, I **commend** you.*

confident, *adj.* self-assured; certain
confidant, *n.* a person in whom one can confide
*I am **confident** that I can trust you as my **confidant**.*

conscience, *n.* the awareness of right and wrong
conscious, *adj.* awake and able to feel and think
*Listen to your **conscience**, and you'll be more **conscious** of right and wrong.*

cooperation, *n.* a working together for a common purpose
corporation, *n.* an organization of people who act as one person

*We need more **cooperation** between the chocolate **corporation** and the peanut butter **corporation.***

continual, *adj.* frequently repeating (but stopping from time to time)

continuous, *adj.* without interruption; never stopping

*The **continual** barking of the dog and the **continuous** banging of the radiator kept them up all night.*

costume, *n.* clothing worn in a play, circus, etc.

custom, *n.* a habit; a usual practice

*Wearing this colorful **costume** on holidays is a **custom** in his country.*

diseased, *adj.* having a sickness or illness or affected by one

deceased, *adj.* dead

*Last time we spoke you told me your cat was **diseased**. Now I'm afraid to ask—is he **deceased**?*

decent, *adj.* proper and respectable

descent, *n.* the action of going down

*Your behavior should be **decent** on our **descent** to Quiet Valley.*

desert, *n.* a hot, dry, sandy region with little plant or animal life

dessert, *n.* the last course of a meal, usually a sweet food

*In the hot **desert**, you can't get a frozen **dessert** or it will melt immediately.*

illicit, *adj.* illegal; not permitted by law

elicit, *v.* to bring out; to draw forth

*The police tried to **elicit** answers about **illicit** drug smuggling.*

emigrate, *v.* to go out of one country to live in another

immigrate, *v.* to enter a country to live there

*I will **emigrate** from Italy so I can **immigrate** into the United States.*

eminent, *adj.* outstanding, notable; distinguished above all others

imminent, *adj.* about to happen; impending; threatening

*The **eminent** professor is aware of an **imminent** disaster if he doesn't hand the papers back before vacation.*

farther, *adv.* at a greater physical distance

further, *adj.* additional; to a more advanced point

*I'll have to travel **farther** to make **further** progress on my research.*

finally, *adv.* at last; in conclusion

finely, *adv.* in a very precise way; in small pieces

***Finally** we found thread spun **finely** enough to sew dolls' clothes.*

formerly, *adv.* in time past; previously

formally, *adv.* in a stiff, proper, polite, or official manner

*The woman who was **formerly** the ambassador came dressed very **formally.***

hearty, *adj.* full of warmth, affection, friendliness, and kindness
hardy, *adj.* strong; robust; tough; able to endure harsh conditions
*I was given a **hearty** welcome by the **hardy** couple.*

human, *adj.* of or relating to human beings
humane, *adj.* showing sympathy, kindness, mercy, and compassion
*A good **human** being is always **humane** to other living things.*

incredible, *adj.* so strange or unusual that it is unbelievable
incredulous, *adj.* feeling doubt or disbelief
*She told such an **incredible** tale, it's no wonder I was **incredulous.***

latter, *adj.* being the second of two things referred to
later, *adj.* coming after the expected time
*I won't say who was **later** to school, but, of Adam and Eric, the **latter** didn't even make lunchtime!*

lay, *v.* to put something down (always followed by a direct object)
lie, *v.* to place oneself in a resting position (never followed by a direct object)
*Do not **lay** your head on the ground when you **lie** on the grass.*

lose, *v.* to misplace; to fail to win
loose, *adj.* not firmly attached
*You will probably **lose** your **loose** tooth any minute.*

magnate, *n.* a person of great wealth or power in a field or activity
magnet, *n.* a piece of metal that attracts or repels iron or steel
*The industrial **magnate** won the award for developing the super **magnet.***

moral, *adj.* good in behavior or character
morale, *n.* the attitude or spirit of a person or a group
*It is **moral** to keep the **morale** of your employees high.*

persecute, *v.* to treat someone cruelly or harmfully again and again
prosecute, *v.* to bring a person before a court of law
*If you try to **persecute** them by withholding their dessert for the third day in a row, I will **prosecute** you for your cruelty.*

personal, *adj.* private; relating to a particular person
personnel, *n.* people working in a business
*He would rather not have the entire **personnel** department know his **personal** problem.*

picture, *n.* a drawing, painting, or photograph

pitcher, *n.* a baseball player who throws the ball to the batter; also a container for holding and pouring liquids
I took a great picture of the pitcher drinking from a pitcher at the end of the game.

precede, *v.* to go in front of someone or something
proceed, *v.* to move forward; to go on with something after stopping
Precede me into the room, so we can proceed with the meeting.

preposition, *adj.* a word that shows the relationship between words
proposition, *n.* a suggested scheme or plan
He made a proposition that we change the preposition from "on" to "in."

quite, *adv.* completely; entirely
quiet, *adj.* making no sound; with little noise; peaceful; still
It has gotten quite noisy at work, and if things don't get quiet, I'll quit.

set, *v.* to put something in a place
sit, *v.* to rest the lower body with the weight off the feet
Set down your packages and sit for a while.

sweet, *adj.* having a pleasant taste like honey or sugar
suite, *n.* connected rooms
In my dream I had a mountain of sweet foods delivered to me in a big hotel suite.

then, *adv.* at that time
than, *conj.* in comparison with
She stuck her tongue out at him, and then he said that he was smarter than she was. What a fight!

thorough, *adj.* all that is needed; complete; perfect
through, *prep.* from one end to the other
Sherlock Holmes conducted a thorough investigation of the crime by searching through every desk in the place.

umpire, *n.* a person who rules on the plays in a sport or game
empire, *n.* a group of countries under one government
On his vacation, the umpire visited the British empire.

Homonyms:

Words That Sound Alike but Are Spelled Differently

Homonyms, or homophones, are words that are spelled differently, have different meanings, but are pronounced alike. Usually they come in pairs. Sometimes they come in triplets. Here are some of the most common.

allowed, *adj.* permitted
aloud, *adv.* out loud; with noise
Strict librarian: *You are not allowed to talk aloud here.*

ant, *n.* tiny insect
aunt, *n.* your parent's sister or your uncle's wife
Uncle: *Look at the little ant climbing on the shoe of your aunt.*

ate, *v.* past tense of "to eat"
eight, *n.* the number between seven and nine
Jet traveler: *Yesterday I ate breakfast at eight p.m.!*

bear, *n.* big, furry animal
bare, *adj.* naked
Shocked zookeeper: *Bear, you're bare! Put your fur on.*

blue, *m.* a color
blew, *v.* past tense of "to blow"
Modern nursery rhyme: *Little Boy Blue really blew his horn.*

break, *v.* to make come apart
brake, *n.* a device for stopping a vehicle

Driving teacher: *Don't press too hard or you'll break the brake.*

bury, *v.* to put something into the earth
berry, *n.* a small, pulpy fruit with seeds
Detective: *Why would the dog bury the berry in the garden?*

capital, *adj.* main, principal, chief
capitol, *n.* the building in which the legislature meets
Tour guide: *In the capital city, you'll visit the capitol building.*

close, *v.* to shut; to block an entrance or opening
clothes, *n.* articles of clothing
Mother: *Close the door to the clothes closet.*

dear, *n.* greatly loved person
deer, *n.* forest animal like a moose or elk
Girlfriend: *Dear, look at that darling deer.*

fair, *adj.* just; impartial; according to accepted rules
fare, *n.* the cost of a ride on a train, bus, plane, etc.
Annoyed bus rider: *I don't think it's fair to charge an extra fare.*

feat, *n.* an act or deed that shows great strength, courage, or skill
feet, *n.* plural of "foot"
Marathon winner: *I owe this great feat to my great feet.*

flew, *v.* past tense of "to fly"
flu, *n.* short for "influenza," a highly contagious disease
Sick pilot: *I flew the plane even though I had the flu.*

flour, *n.* fine, ground grain used for baking
flower, *n.* the blossom or bloom on a plant
Fancy baker: *This flour is made of flower petals.*

heard, *v.* past tense of the verb "to hear"
herd, *n.* a group of large animals like cattle or sheep
Angry cowboy: *I heard what you said about my herd!*

he'll, contraction for "he will"
heal, *v.* to make well; cure
heel, *n.* the rounded, rear part of the human foot, below the ankle
Foot doctor's nurse: *He'll try to heal your sore heel.*

here, *adv.* at or in this place

hear, *v.* to receive sounds in the ear
Telephone repairer: *Here, see if you can hear with this phone.*

lone, *adj.* alone
loan, *n.* a sum of money lent at interest
Banker: *Do you think you're the lone person who needs a loan?*

mail, *n.* letters or packages sent through the post office
male, *n.* a man
Post office rule: *A mail carrier can be male or female.*

Maine, *n.* a state in New England.
main, *adj.* the greatest in size or importance; chief; principal
mane, *n.* long, heavy hair around the neck of some animals
New England stable owner: *In Maine, the main thing is to brush the horse's mane regularly.*

meet, *v.* to make the acquaintance of someone
meat, *n.* flesh of animals used as food
Strict vegetarian: *I don't want to meet someone who eats meat.*

no, *adv.* certainly not; not so
know, *v.* to be certain of the facts; to understand clearly
Student who didn't study: *No, I don't know the answer.*

our, *pron.* belongs to us
hour, *n.* sixty minutes

Noisy kids: *Our mother told us to be quiet for an hour.*

pain, *n.* a feeling of hurt, suffering, or physical distress
pane, *n.* a sheet of glass placed in a window
Angry house owner: *What a pain! My window pane is broken.*

pale, *adj.* without healthy color
pail, *n.* a round, open container for carrying water, sand, etc.
Storyteller: *Jack and Jill turned pale when they lost their pail.*

pear, *n.* a fruit shaped like a bell
pair, *n.* a set of two things
Math teacher: *One pear and one pear equal a pair of pears.*

piece, *n.* a part of something
peace, *n.* freedom from war or fighting; calmness
History museum guide: *This piece of paper is the peace treaty.*

plane, *n.* an airplane
plain, *n.* an area of flat land; or *adj.* ordinary
Bored pilot: *We're landing the plane on the plain, flat plain again.*

pray, *v.* to ask or beg for something
prey, *v.* to hunt a living thing
Man lost in woods: *I pray that an animal doesn't prey on me.*

principal, *n.* the head of a school
principle, *n.* a rule of personal behavior

Proud pupil: *Our principal is a person of very high principle.*

reign, *n.* the period that a monarch (king or queen) rules
rein, *n.* straps attached to the sides of a horse's mouth for riding
rain, *n.* drops of water that fall from the sky
Royal historian: *During her reign, the queen always held the rein during a heavy rain.*

roll, *n.* a list of names
role, *n.* a part in a play or movie
Movie director: *Call the roll of people who want to play this role.*

sail, *n.* canvas that catches the wind and causes a boat to move
sale, *n.* the selling of goods for less than the usual cost
Budget-minded boat owner: *I'll get a new sail when they're on sale.*

seen, *v.* past participle of "to see"
scene, *n.* an episode, especially in a play, movie, or television show
One movie fan to another: *You should have seen that scene!*

sent, *v.* past tense of "to send"
cent, *n.* a penny
scent, *n.* an odor, smell, or aroma
Girl: *I sent my boyfriend with a cent to buy me a pretty scent.*

soar, *v.* fly upward
sore, *adj.* painful
Baby bird: *After I soar over the mountains, my wings are sore.*

some, *adj.* a portion; a few, or re-markable; striking
sum, *n.* amount of money
Student looking at a long addition problem: *Some kids would say that's some big sum!*

son, *n.* male child
sun, *n.* the hot, bright star that is the center of our solar system
Father: *Son, our closest star is the sun.*

stare, *v.* to look at for a long time
stair, *n.* a step
Gentleman: *I can't help but stare at the lovely lady on the stair.*

stationary, *adj.* not moving
stationery, *n.* writing paper, en-velopes, etc.
Mother to restless child: *Stay sta-tionary in the stationery store.*

steal, *v.* to take something with-out permission
steel, *n.* an alloy of iron mixed with carbon
Judge to thief: *You are guilty of try-ing to steal the steel.*

tale, *n.* a story
tail, *n.* part of an animal's body that sticks out from its main part
Jungle guide: *I'll tell you an amazing tale about a tiger's tail.*

there, *adv.* at or in that place
their, *pron.* belonging to them
they're, contraction for "they are"

Eyewitness to police: *They're over there in their secret hideout.*

threw, *v.* past tense of "to throw"
through, *prep.* in one side of something and out the other
Sportscaster: *He threw the ball through the scoreboard!*

to, *prep.* toward
two, *n.* and *adj.* the number be-tween one and three
too, *adv.* also; in addition; also, more than enough
One movie fan to another: *I went to the movies and saw two films, too.*

wait, *n.* to stop or stay in place, expecting something to happen
weight, *n.* the heaviness of something
Trainer to athlete: *Wait a minute. I need to know your weight.*

waste, *v.* to make poor use of something
waist, *n.* part of the body around the middle
Dieter: *I hate to waste food, but it will all end up on my waist.*

way, *n.* the form or method of doing something
weigh, *v.* to find out how heavy something is
Scale demonstrator: *This is the way you weigh yourself.*

week, *n.* seven days
weak, *adj.* not strong

Overworked student: *At the end of each week I feel weak.*

where, *adv.* in what place
wear, *v.* to have clothes on the body
Shopper: *Where would I ever wear a dress like that?*

whether, *conj.* it; either
weather, *n.* the condition of the atmosphere
Meteorologist: *I don't know whether tomorrow's weather will be good or bad.*

which, *pron.* a word that asks questions about people and things
witch, *n.* a woman with evil supernatural powers
Halloween judge: *Which of the witch costumes is ugliest?*

whole, *adj.* complete; entire

hole, *n.* an opening in the ground
Boss to ditchdigger: *Dig this hole for the whole day.*

won, *v.* past tense of "to win"
one, *n.* and *adj.* the first and lowest whole number
Sportscaster: *The team won only one game the whole season.*

write, *v.* to make letters and words with a pen or pencil
right, *adj.* the opposite of left; also, correct
Penmanship teacher: *Write with your left or right hand. They're both right.*

Idioms:

When Words Mean More Than They Say

An idiom is a phrase with a special meaning. Often the meaning has very little (or absolutely nothing) to do with the actual meanings of the words taken one by one. For example, if you tell someone she just "laid an egg," you don't mean that she's a hen. You mean that she just suffered a big failure. "Laid an egg" used this way is an idiom.

If you hear or see an idiom that you don't understand, try looking the key word up in a dictionary. For instance, if you want to know what a "skeleton in the closet" means, look up "skeleton." You'll find that the idiom means having a secret that you don't want anyone to find out.

If the expression isn't in the dictionary, you might find a book in your school or local library that explains idioms.

Here are some common idioms and their explanations:

- *The teacher's bark is worse than his bite, so don't worry.*
  (What he says sounds much worse than what he'll do.)

- *If I'm wrong about this, I'll eat my words.*
  (If I made a mistake, I'll admit it.)

- *That new kid really gets under my skin.*
  (He really annoys me a lot.)

- *After her big science experiment fizzled, she had egg on her face.*
  (She was very embarrassed in public.)

- *We've got to help each other because we're all in the same boat.*
  (We're in the same bad situation together.)

- *This new song you wrote is going to knock their socks off!*
(It will amaze and excite them in a way they didn't expect.)

- *With this evidence against him, he won't have a leg to stand on.*
(He won't have any facts to support his case.)

- *Uh-oh! Looks like we're out of the frying pan and into the fire!*
(We're going from a bad situation into an even worse one.)

- *Do it yourself, and don't try to pass the buck on to me.*
(Don't try to shift the responsibility.)

- *The bus is leaving, so you'd better shake a leg.*
(Hurry up. Move fast.)

- *No matter what they say to convince you to do it, stick to your guns.*
(Hold on to your own ideals, even when people try to persuade you to change.)

- *He swallowed my excuse hook, line, and sinker.*
(He believed everything I said without question or doubt.)

Clichés

Some idioms are also clichés. A cliché (pronounced "clee-SHAY") is a popular saying that is used so often by so many people that it gets overused. Most good writers and speakers avoid using clichés and try to make up new, imaginative expressions of their own.

Avoiding Sexist Language

In the past, the noun **man** referred to all human beings regardless of whether they were men or women. **Mankind** was used to mean humankind. In the same way, the masculine pronouns **he, his, him**, and **himself** referred not only to boys and men, but also to girls and women.

> *Tell a person who wants to succeed that he must work hard.*

> *Everyone should take out his spelling book.*

> *Throughout history, man has struggled to keep himself free.*

Today, many writers and speakers try to avoid sentences like those. After all, shouldn't girls work hard, too? Unless it's an all-boys school, shouldn't the girls take out their spelling books? And since the beginning of time, haven't girls and women fought for freedom, too?

Ways to Avoid Sexist Language

- Find new ways to include feminine pronouns (**she, her, herself**) along with the masculine pronouns.

> *Tell a person who wants to succeed that **he or she** must work hard.*

> *Everyone should take out **his or her** spelling book.*

But it can get awkward and wordy if you always try to include both sexes equally in everything you write.

> *If a student wants to audition for the play, he or she should bring his or her script to the auditorium after his or her last class today.*

■ A way of solving this kind of **he/she, him/her, his/her** problem is to use neutral nouns and pronouns or to use plural nouns and pronouns instead of singular ones:

> *Anyone who wants to succeed should work hard.*
>
> *Class, take out your spelling books.*
>
> *Throughout history, people have struggled to keep themselves free.*
>
> *Students auditioning for the play should bring their scripts to the auditorium after their last classes today.*

■ Some people are using a newly created pronoun, **s/he**, to stand for **she** and **he**.

> *If a person wishes to enter the contest, **s/he** should submit an entry form immediately.*

But it's not clear yet if enough people will use **s/he** for it to become an accepted and natural part of our language.

■ Many people prefer to drop the feminine noun altogether or use a new form. For example, **actress, fireman**, and **mailman** become **actor, firefighter**, and **mail carrier.**

Initials, Acronyms, and Abbreviations

Initials

Initials are a kind of abbreviation. Sometimes expressions or the names of things are known by their initials (their first letters). These initials take the place of the whole name or word. Here are some of the most common:

Common Initials	
A.D.	Anno Domini (Latin for "in the year of our Lord"); any year from 1 on (*The king was born in A.D. 1640.*)
a.m. or A.M.	*ante meridiem* (Latin for "before noon"); the time from midnight to noon
ASAP	As Soon As Possible
ASPCA	American Society for the Prevention of Cruelty to Animals
B.A.	Bachelor of Arts; a college degree
B.C.	Before Christ; any year before the year 1. British Columbia
B.C.E.	Before the Common Era; any time before the year 1
B.S.	Bachelor of Science; a college degree
C	Celsius; a way to measure temperature(See also **F**)
C.E.	Common Era; any time after the year 1
CD-ROM	Compact Disk-Read Only Memory
CIA	Central Intelligence Agency; branch of the federal government that gathers information about other countries
C.O.D.	Collect (or cash) on Delivery when the package arrives
CTW	Children's Television Workshop
D.A.	District Attorney
D.C.	District of Columbia; as in Washington, D.C.
e.g.	*exempli gratia* (Latin for "for example")
ERA	Equal Rights Amendment
etc.	*et cetera* (Latin for "and so forth," "and others")
F	Fahrenheit; a measurement of temperature (see also **C**)

FBI	Federal Bureau of Investigation; branch of federal government that investigates crime
GI	Government Issue; nickname for a soldier (Origin: The government issued everything a soldier needed—uniform, weapons, etc.)
HQ	Headquarters
IRS	Internal Revenue Service; the federal government agency that collects income taxes
M.A.	Master of Arts; a college degree
M.D.	Doctor of Medicine; a medical doctor's degree
m.p.h.	miles per hour
MIA	Missing in Action; a lost fighter during war
MTV	Music Television
NAACP	National Association for the Advancement of Colored People
N.B.A.	National Basketball Association
N.H.L.	National Hockey League
N.F.L.	National Football League
p.m. or P.M.	*post meridiem* (Latin for "after noon"); noon to midnight
P.O.	Post Office
PA	Public Address; loudspeaker system
PC	Personal Computer
POW	Prisoner of War; a fighter captured by the enemy in a war
P.S.	Postscript; a note written after the close of a letter
R.N.	Registered Nurse
R.I.P.	Rest in Peace; often written on a gravestone
RR	Railroad
RSVP	*Répondez s'il vous plaît;* French for "Please Respond," often put on invitations
RV	Recreational Vehicle
SAT	Scholastic Assessment Test; a college entrance exam
TLC	Tender Loving Care; an expression
UFO	Unidentified Flying Object
UN or U.N.	United Nations
VIP	Very Important Person

Acronyms

An acronym is a kind of abbreviation. It is a word made out of the first letters of other words. Acronyms never have periods, and they are almost always written out in all capital letters. Here are some of the most common:

Common Acronyms	
AIDS	Acquired Immune Deficiency Syndrome
AWOL	Absent WithOut Leave
CORE	Congress of Racial Equality
HUD	Housing and Urban Development
JEEP	(G.P. vehicle) General Purpose
MADD	Mothers Against Drunk Driving
SADD	Students Against Drunk Driving
MASH	Mobile Army Surgical Hospital
NASA	National Aeronautics and Space Administration
NATO	North Atlantic Treaty Organization
NOW	National Organization for Women
OPEC	Organization of Petroleum Exporting Countries
PIN	Personal Identification Number
RADAR	Radio Detecting and Ranging
SALT	Strategic Arms Limitation Talks
SCUBA	Self-contained Underwater Breathing Apparatus
SNAFU	Situation Normal, All Fouled Up
SONAR	Sound navigation ranging
SWAK	Sealed With A Kiss
SWAT	Special Weapons Action Team or Special Weapons and Tactics
UNESCO	United Nations Educational, Scientific, and Cultural Organization
UNICEF	United Nations International Children's Education Fund
VISTA	Volunteers in Service to America
WAC	Women's Army Corps
WHO	World Health Organization
ZIP	Zone Improvement Plan

Abbreviations

To speed up your writing, you may sometimes use a shortened form (abbreviation) of a word or phrase. You usually put a period at the end of an abbreviation, but sometimes you don't. If in doubt, check the list on pages 294–295 or your dictionary.

Use postal abbreviations on addresses in letters and on envelopes. Use the standard abbreviations for all formal writing.

State Abbreviations

	Postal	Standard		Postal	Standard
Alabama	AL	Ala.	Montana	MT	Mont.
Alaska	AK	Alaska	Nebraska	NE	Neb.
Arizona	AZ	Ariz.	Nevada	NV	Nev.
Arkansas	AR	Ark.	New Hampshire	NH	N.H.
California	CA	Calif.	New Jersey	NJ	N.J.
Colorado	CO	Colo.	New Mexico	NM	N.M.
Connecticut	CT	Conn.	New York	NY	N.Y.
Delaware	DE	Del.	North Carolina	NC	N.C.
Dist. of Columbia	DC	D.C.	North Dakota	ND	N.D.
Florida	FL	Fla.	Ohio	OH	Ohio
Georgia	GA	Ga.	Oklahoma	OK	Okla.
Guam	GU	Guam	Oregon	OR	Ore.
Hawaii	III	Hawaii	Pennsylvania	PA	Pa.
Idaho	ID	Idaho	Puerto Rico	PR	P.R.
Illinois	IL	Ill.	Rhode Island	RI	R.I.
Indiana	IN	Ind.	South Carolina	SC	S.C.
Iowa	IA	Iowa	South Dakota	SD	S.D.
Kansas	KS	Kan.	Tennessee	TN	Tenn.
Kentucky	KY	Ky.	Texas	TX	Texas
Louisiana	LA	La.	Utah	UT	Utah
Maine	ME	Maine	Vermont	VT	Vt.
Maryland	MD	Md.	Virginia	VA	Va.
Massachusetts	MA	Mass.	Virgin Islands	VI	V.I.
Michigan	MI	Mich.	Washington	WA	Wash.
Minnesota	MN	Minn.	West Virginia	WV	W.Va.
Mississippi	MS	Miss.	Wisconsin	WI	Wis.
Missouri	MO	Mo.	Wyoming	WY	Wyo.

How to Use Abbreviations

Abbreviations are never used as words by themselves. They always go along with other words or names.

*They live on a pretty **street.***

*Deliver this to 34 Oakdale **St.***

*Tomorrow we climb the **mountain.***

*Few people have ever climbed **Mt.** Everest.*

*It can be very cold in **February.***

*He was born on **Feb.** 14, 1972.*

Common Abbreviations

Here are other common abbreviations. Almost all end with periods.

Common Abbreviations

Adm.	Admiral	**Col.**	Colonel
anon.	anonymous	**Comdr.**	Commander
apt.	apartment	**cont.**	continued
assoc.	associate	**Corp.**	Corporation
asst.	assistant	**Dec.**	December
atty.	attorney	**Dept.**	Department
Aug.	August	**Dr.**	Doctor; Drive
Ave.	avenue	**etc.**	and others, and so forth
Bldg.	Building		(Latin: **et cetera**)
Blvd.	Boulevard		Note: Always put a comma in
Capt.	Captain		front of **etc.**
cm.	centimeters	**Feb.**	February
Cpl.	Corporal	**ft.**	foot (feet)
Co.	Company	**Gov.**	Governor

in.	inches	**Pky. or**	Parkway
Inc.	Incorporated	**Pkwy.**	
Jan.	January	**Pres.**	President
Jr.	junior	**Prof.**	Professor
kg.	kilogram	**pt.**	pints
km.	kilometer	**Pvt.**	Private
lat.	latitude	**qt.**	quarts
lb., lbs.	pound, pounds	**Rd.**	Road
long.	longitude	**Rep.**	Representative
Ltd.	Limited	**Rev.**	Reverend
Maj.	Major	**Sen.**	Senator
misc.	miscellaneous	**Sept.**	September
ml.	milliliter(s)	**Sgt.**	Sergeant
Mt.	Mountain; Mount	**Sr.**	Senior; Sister
No.	number; north	**St.**	Street; Saint
Nov.	November	**supt.**	superintendent
Oct.	October	**vol.**	volume
oz.	ounces	**vs. or v.**	versus, opposing
p.; pp.	page; pages	**yd.; yds.**	yard; yards
Ph.D.	Doctor of Philosophy		

If the last word in a sentence is an abbreviation with a period, you don't have to use another period to end the sentence.

For additional information, write to Freedman Pharmaceuticals, Inc.

Index

Religions, capitalization of, 84
Reports, 210
  bibliographies in, 204-206
  book, 160–170
  clear information in, 229–233
  outlines for, 214–215
  research for, 212
  science, 184–190
  social studies, 191–203
Research
  brainstorming for, 212–213
  for writing assignment,
    211–212
Research topic report
  parts of, 187–189
  samples of, 188, 189
  tips for writing, 186–187
Resolution, 243, 245
Reviews, 210
Rhymes, 239–240
Rhyming patterns, 240–241
Run-on sentences, 60–61
  avoiding, 226–227

S

Salutation
  for business letter, 143–144
  capitalization in, 80
  of friendly letter, 126–127
Scenes, 247–248
Science report
  on experiment, 184–185
  on person, 184, 190

research for, 212
  on research topic, 184,
    186–189
Script, format of, 246
Scripture, capitalization of, 84
Scriptwriting, 245–249
Seasons, capitalization of, 80
Second-person, subject-verb
  agreement with, 62, 63
Second-person pronoun, 23
Sections, numbering of, 271
Semiblock format, 141
Semicolon, 102–103
  in compound sentence, 59
  in run-on sentence, 61
  in series, 103
Sentence
  adjectives in, 43
  building, 217–219
  capitalization of first word in,
    76
  complex, 59
  compound, 58–59
  exclamatory, 90
  fragments, 59–60
  imperative, exclamation
    points with, 90
  kinds of, 57
  paragraphs and, 219–220
  parentheses in, 94
  periods in, 95
  personal pronoun as subject
    of, 18

W